Fourth Edition

NorthStar 1

Reading & Writing

Authors: John Beaumont
A. Judith Yancey

Series Editors: Frances Boyd
Carol Numrich

NorthStar: Reading & Writing Level 1, Fourth Edition

Copyright © 2020, 2015, 2009, 2004 by Pearson Education, Inc.
All rights reserved.

No part of this publication may be reproduced, stored in a retrieval system, or transmitted in any form or by any means, electronic, mechanical, photocopying, recording, or otherwise, without the prior permission of the publisher.

Pearson Education, 221 River St, Hoboken, NJ 07030

Staff credits: The people who made up the *NorthStar: Reading & Writing Level 1, Fourth Edition* team, representing content creation, design, marketing, manufacturing, multimedia, project management, publishing, rights management, and testing, are Pietro Alongi, Stephanie Callahan, Gina DiLillo, Tracey Cataldo, Dave Dickey, Warren Fishbach, Sarah Hand, Lucy Hart, Gosia Jaros-White, Stefan Machura, Linda Moser, Dana Pinter, Karen Quinn, Katarzyna Starzynska - Kosciuszko, Paula Van Ells, Claire Van Poperin, Joseph Vella, Peter West, Autumn Westphal, Natalia Zaremba, and Marcin Zimny.

Project consultant: Debbie Sistino
Text composition: ElectraGraphics, Inc.
Development editing: Barefoot Editorial Services, Inc.
Cover design: Studio Montage

Library of Congress Cataloging-in-Publication Data

A Catalog record for the print edition is available from the Library of Congress.

Printed in the United States of America

ISBN-13: 978-0-13-523261-3 (Student Book with Digital Resources)
ISBN-10: 0-13-523261-9 (Student Book with Digital Resources)

    2 2019

ISBN-13: 978-0-13-5222701-5 (Student Book with MyEnglishLab Online Workbook and Resources)
ISBN-10: 0-13-522701-1 (Student Book with MyEnglishLab Online Workbook and Resources)

    2 2019

CONTENTS

Welcome to *NorthStar*, Fourth Edition iv

Scope and Sequence xiv

Acknowledgments/Reviewers xviii

UNIT 1 Green Spaces 2

UNIT 2 Art for Everyone 26

UNIT 3 What's It Worth to You? 50

UNIT 4 Open for Business 70

UNIT 5 What Are You Afraid Of? 94

UNIT 6 What an Adventure! 118

UNIT 7 What Number Are You? 142

UNIT 8 Too Young to Go Pro? 166

Expand Vocabulary 190

Academic Word List Vocabulary 191

Grammar Book References 192

Credits 193

WELCOME TO NORTHSTAR

A Letter from the Series Editors

We welcome you to the 4th edition of *NorthStar Reading & Writing Level 1*.

Engaging content, integrated skills, and critical thinking continue to be the touchstones of the series. For more than 20 years *NorthStar* has engaged and motivated students through contemporary, authentic topics. Our online component builds on the last edition by offering new and updated activities.

Since its first edition, *NorthStar* has been rigorous in its approach to critical thinking by systematically engaging students in tasks and activities that prepare them to move into high-level academic courses. The cognitive domains of Bloom's taxonomy provide the foundation for the critical thinking activities. Students develop the skills of analysis and evaluation and the ability to synthesize and summarize information from multiple sources. The capstone of each unit, the final writing or speaking task, supports students in the application of all academic, critical thinking, and language skills that are the focus of unit.

The new edition introduces additional academic skills for 21st century success: note-taking and presentation skills. There is also a focus on learning outcomes based on the Global Scale of English (GSE), an emphasis on the application of skills, and a new visual design. These refinements are our response to research in the field of language learning in addition to feedback from educators who have taught from our previous editions.

NorthStar has pioneered and perfected the blending of academic content and academic skills in an English Language series. Read on for a comprehensive overview of this new edition. As you and your students explore *NorthStar*, we wish you a great journey.

Carol Numrich and Frances Boyd, the editors

New for the FOURTH EDITION

New and Updated Themes

The new edition features one new theme per level (i.e., one new unit per book), with updated content and skills throughout the series. Current and thought-provoking topics presented in a variety of genres promote intellectual stimulation. The real-world-inspired content engages students, links them to language use outside the classroom, and encourages personal expression and critical thinking.

Learning Outcomes and Assessments

All unit skills, vocabulary, and grammar points are connected to GSE objectives to ensure effective progression of learning throughout the series. Learning outcomes are present at the opening and closing of each unit to clearly mark what is covered in the unit and encourage both pre- and post-unit self-reflection. A variety of assessment tools, including online diagnostic, formative, and summative assessments and a flexible gradebook aligned with clearly identified unit learning outcomes, allow teachers to individualize instruction and track student progress.

Note-Taking as a Skill in Every Unit

Grounded in the foundations of the Cornell Method of note-taking, the new note-taking practice is structured to allow students to reflect on and organize their notes, focusing on the most important points. Students are instructed, throughout the unit, on the most effective way to apply their notes to a classroom task, as well as encouraged to analyze and reflect on their growing note-taking skills.

Explicit Skill Instruction and Fully-Integrated Practice

Concise presentations and targeted practice in print and online prepare students for academic success. Language skills are highlighted in each unit, providing students with multiple, systematic exposures to language forms and structures in a variety of contexts. Academic and language skills in each unit are applied clearly and deliberately in the culminating writing or presentation task.

Scaffolded Critical Thinking

Activities within the unit are structured to follow the stages of Bloom's taxonomy from *remember* to *create*. The use of APPLY throughout the unit highlights culminating activities that allow students to use the skills being practiced in a free and authentic manner. Sections that are focused on developing critical thinking are marked with 🔍 to highlight their critical focus.

Explicit Focus on the Academic Word List

AWL words are highlighted at the end of the unit and in a master list at the end of the book.

The Pearson Practice English App

The **Pearson Practice English App** allows students on the go to complete vocabulary and grammar activities, listen to audio, and watch video.

ExamView

ExamView Test Generator allows teachers to customize assessments by reordering or editing existing questions, selecting test items from a bank, or writing new questions.

MyEnglishLab

New and revised online supplementary practice maps to the updates in the student book for this edition.

THE NORTHSTAR UNIT

1 FOCUS ON THE TOPIC

Each unit begins with an eye-catching unit opener spread that draws students into the topic. The learning outcomes are written in simple, student-friendly language to allow for self-assessment. Focus on the Topic questions connect to the unit theme and get students to think critically by making inferences and predicting the content of the unit.

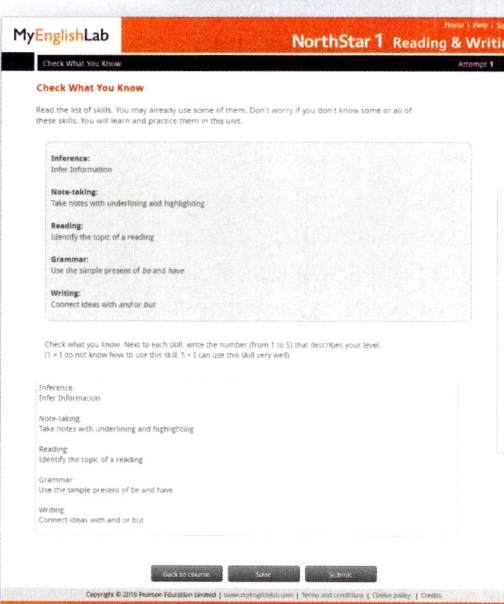

MyEnglishLab

The "Check What You Know" pre-unit diagnostic checklist provides a short self-assessment based on each unit's GSE-aligned learning outcomes to support the students in building an awareness of their own skill levels and to enable teachers to target instruction to their students' specific needs.

2 FOCUS ON READING

A vocabulary exercise introduces words that appear in the readings, encourages students to guess the meanings of the words from context, and connects to the theme presented in the final writing task.

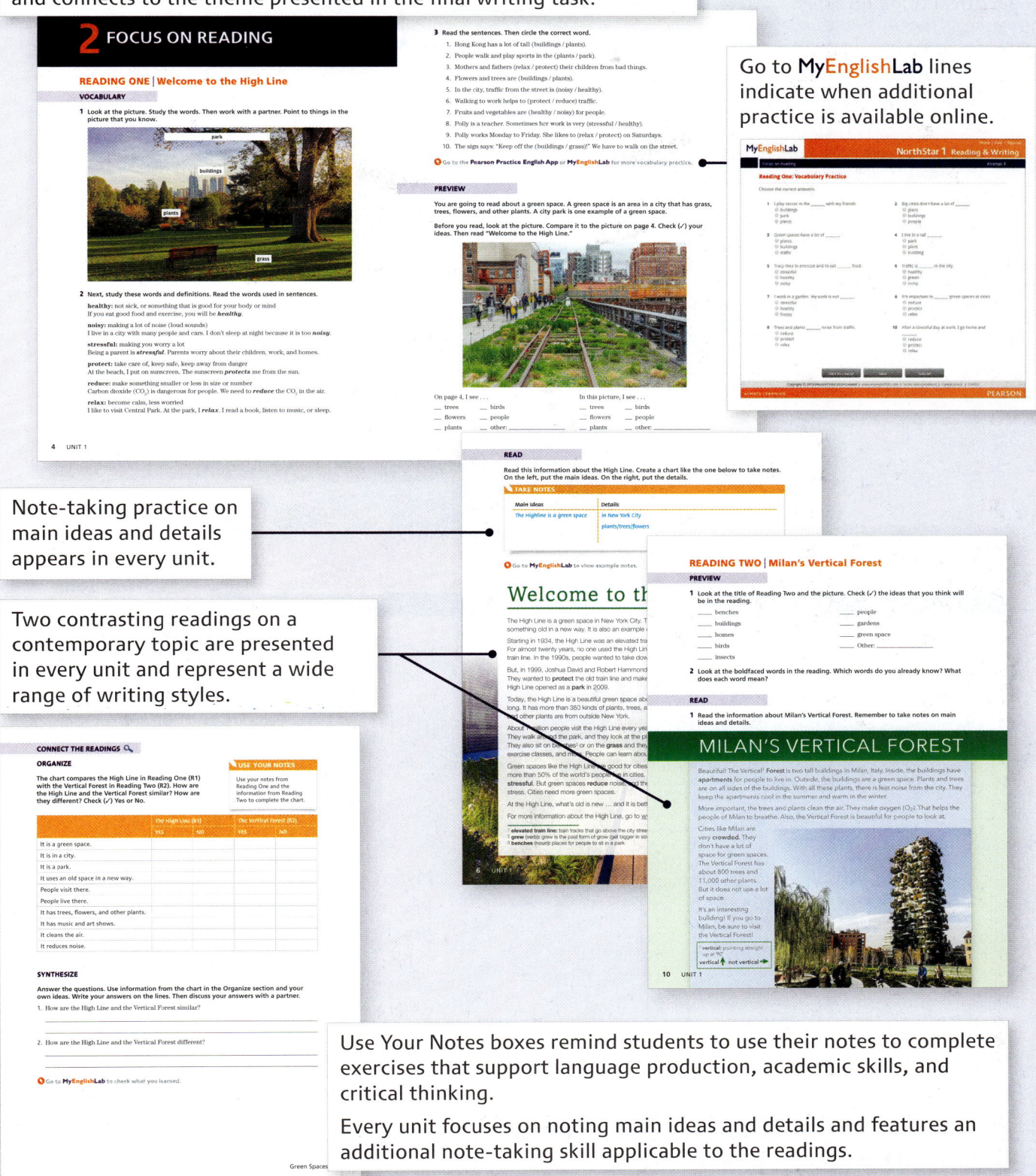

Note-taking practice on main ideas and details appears in every unit.

Two contrasting readings on a contemporary topic are presented in every unit and represent a wide range of writing styles.

Go to MyEnglishLab lines indicate when additional practice is available online.

Use Your Notes boxes remind students to use their notes to complete exercises that support language production, academic skills, and critical thinking.

Every unit focuses on noting main ideas and details and features an additional note-taking skill applicable to the readings.

The NorthStar Unit   vii

EXPLICIT SKILL INSTRUCTION AND PRACTICE

Step-by-step instructions and practice guide students to move beyond the literal meaning of the text. 🔍 highlights activities that help build critical thinking skills.

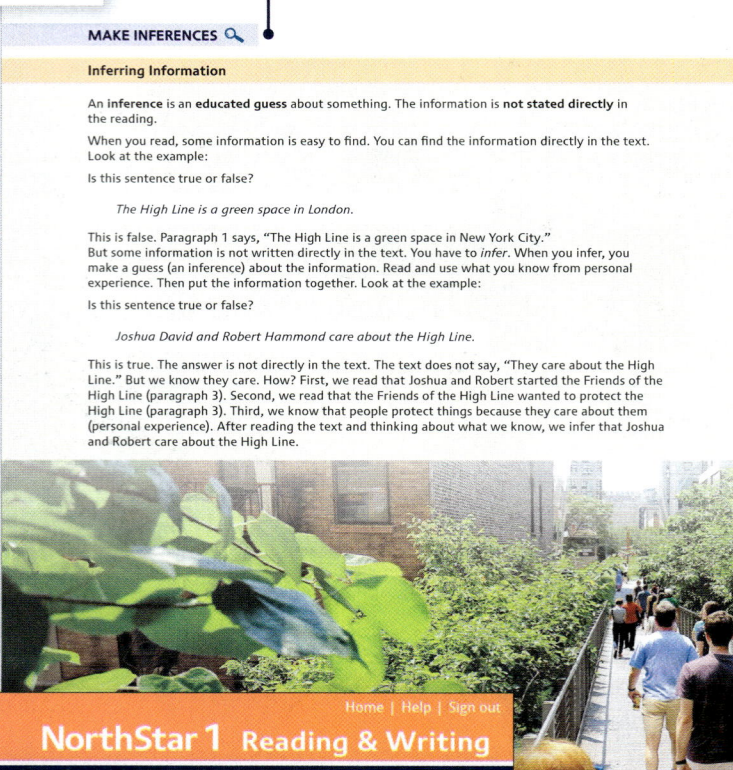

MAKE INFERENCES 🔍

Inferring Information

An **inference** is an **educated guess** about something. The information is **not stated directly** in the reading.

When you read, some information is easy to find. You can find the information directly in the text. Look at the example:

Is this sentence true or false?

The High Line is a green space in London.

This is false. Paragraph 1 says, "The High Line is a green space in New York City." But some information is not written directly in the text. You have to *infer*. When you infer, you make a guess (an inference) about the information. Read and use what you know from personal experience. Then put the information together. Look at the example:

Is this sentence true or false?

Joshua David and Robert Hammond care about the High Line.

This is true. The answer is not directly in the text. The text does not say, "They care about the High Line." But we know they care. How? First, we read that Joshua and Robert started the Friends of the High Line (paragraph 3). Second, we read that the Friends of the High Line wanted to protect the High Line (paragraph 3). Third, we know that people protect things because they care about them (personal experience). After reading the text and thinking about what we know, we infer that Joshua and Robert care about the High Line.

MyEnglishLab

Home | Help | Sign out

NorthStar 1 Reading & Writing

Focus on Reading — Attempt **1**

Reading Practice: Identifying the Topic

Read the passage. Then choose the correct answer to the question.

The Green Greens

Greta and Gary Green live in Fresno, California. Gary is a teacher, and Greta is a doctor. Gary and Greta have two children, Ivy and Leif. The Greens teach their children to love nature.

For the Greens, their home is a green space. They have a lot of plants. Inside the house, plants clean the air. Outside the house, trees reduce noise from traffic. The Greens have a lot of flowers and vegetables in a big garden. The family eats the vegetables.

Outside the house, the Greens also have animals. They have chickens, and they have bees bees also help the flowers and plants in the garden. The Greens have a cow and two goats grass and give the family milk to drink.

Everyone in the Green family helps to take care of their plants and animals. The Greens lo

1 What is the topic of the article?
- ○ Green spaces in California
- ○ The Green family's home
- ○ Vegetable gardens
- ○ Crowded cities

Back to course | Save | Submit

MyEnglishLab

Key reading skills are reinforced and practiced in new contexts. Autograded skills-based activities provide instant scores, allowing teachers and students to identify where improvement is needed.

3 FOCUS ON WRITING

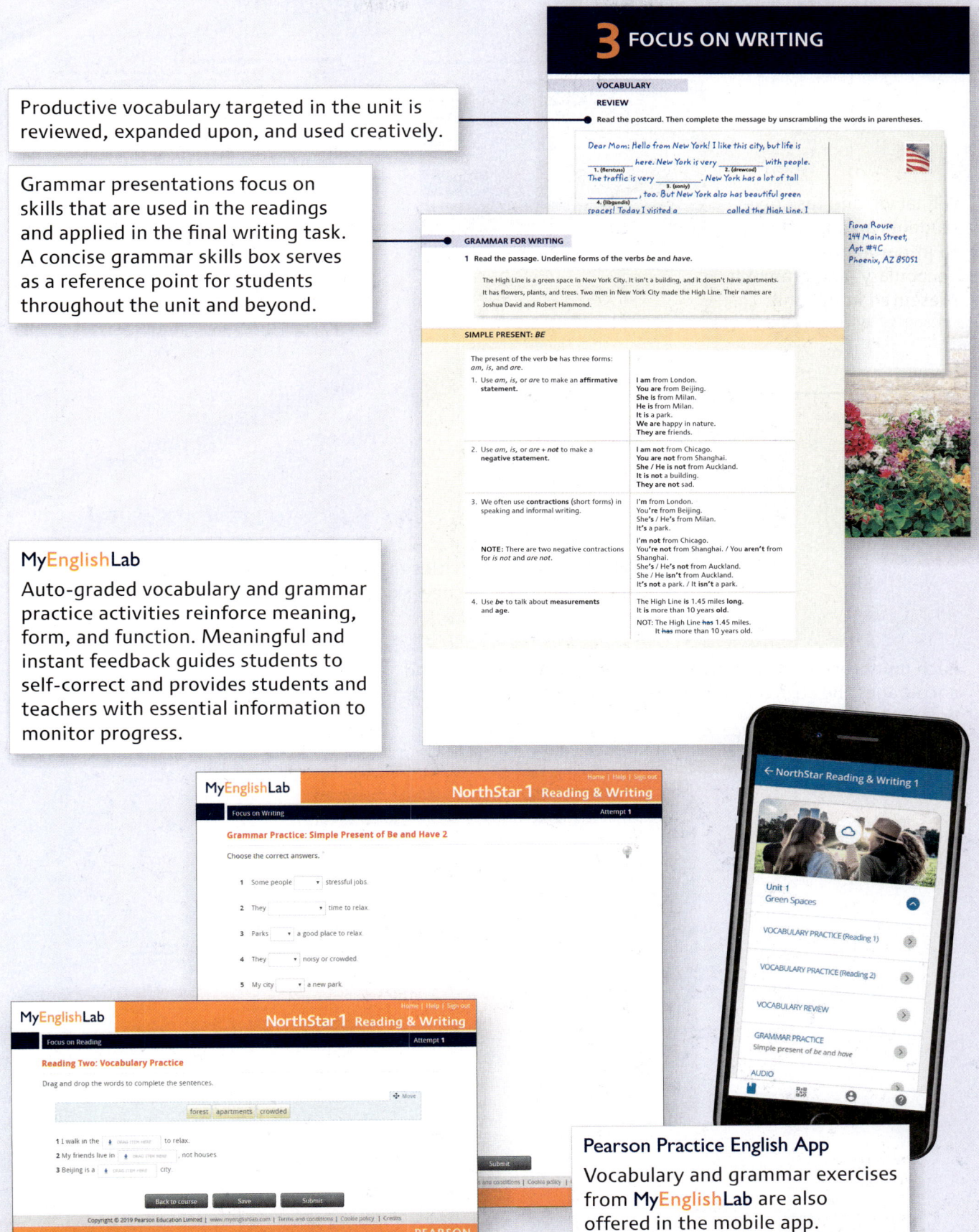

Productive vocabulary targeted in the unit is reviewed, expanded upon, and used creatively.

Grammar presentations focus on skills that are used in the readings and applied in the final writing task. A concise grammar skills box serves as a reference point for students throughout the unit and beyond.

MyEnglishLab
Auto-graded vocabulary and grammar practice activities reinforce meaning, form, and function. Meaningful and instant feedback guides students to self-correct and provides students and teachers with essential information to monitor progress.

Pearson Practice English App
Vocabulary and grammar exercises from MyEnglishLab are also offered in the mobile app.

The NorthStar Unit ix

A TASK-BASED APPROACH TO PROCESS WRITING

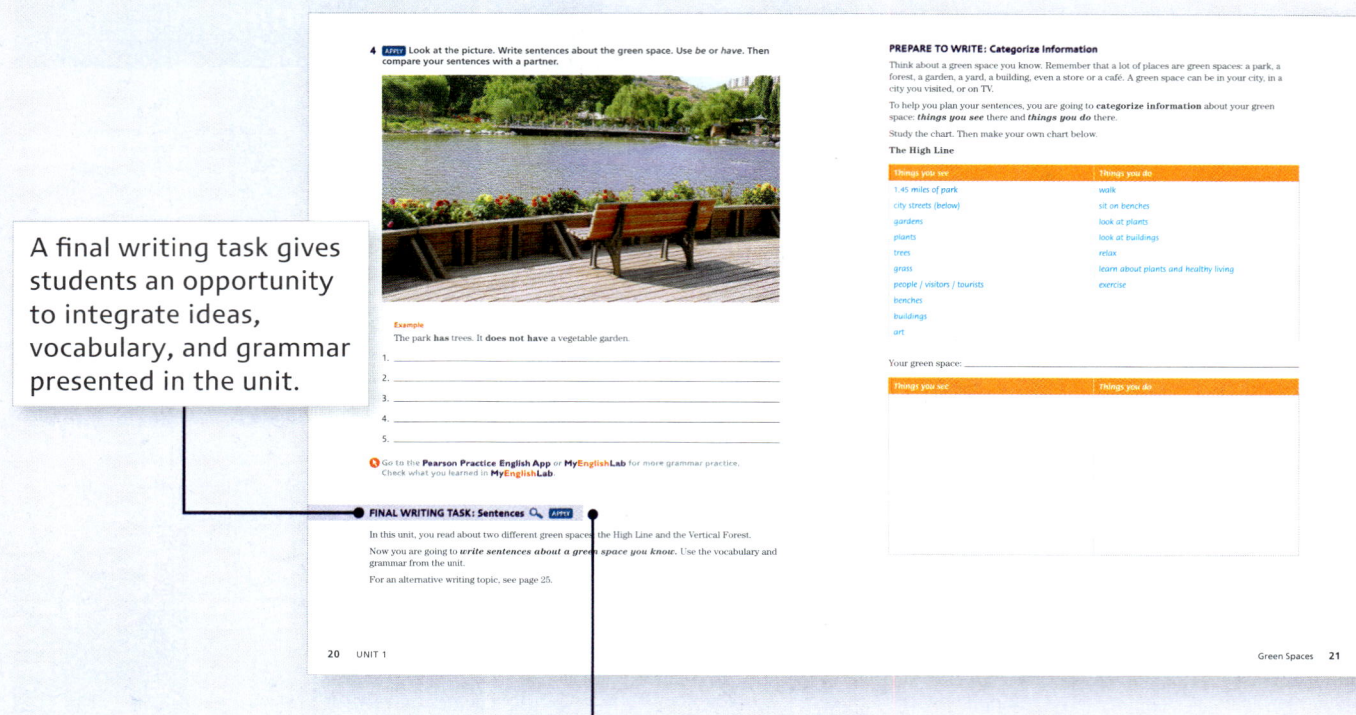

A final writing task gives students an opportunity to integrate ideas, vocabulary, and grammar presented in the unit.

APPLY calls out activities that get students to use new skills in a productive task.

Each unit presents different stages of the writing process and encourages the structured development of writing skills both practical and academic.

The NorthStar Unit

Students continue through the writing process to learn revision techniques that help them move toward coherence and unity in their writing. Finally, students edit their work with the aid of a checklist that focuses on essential outcomes.

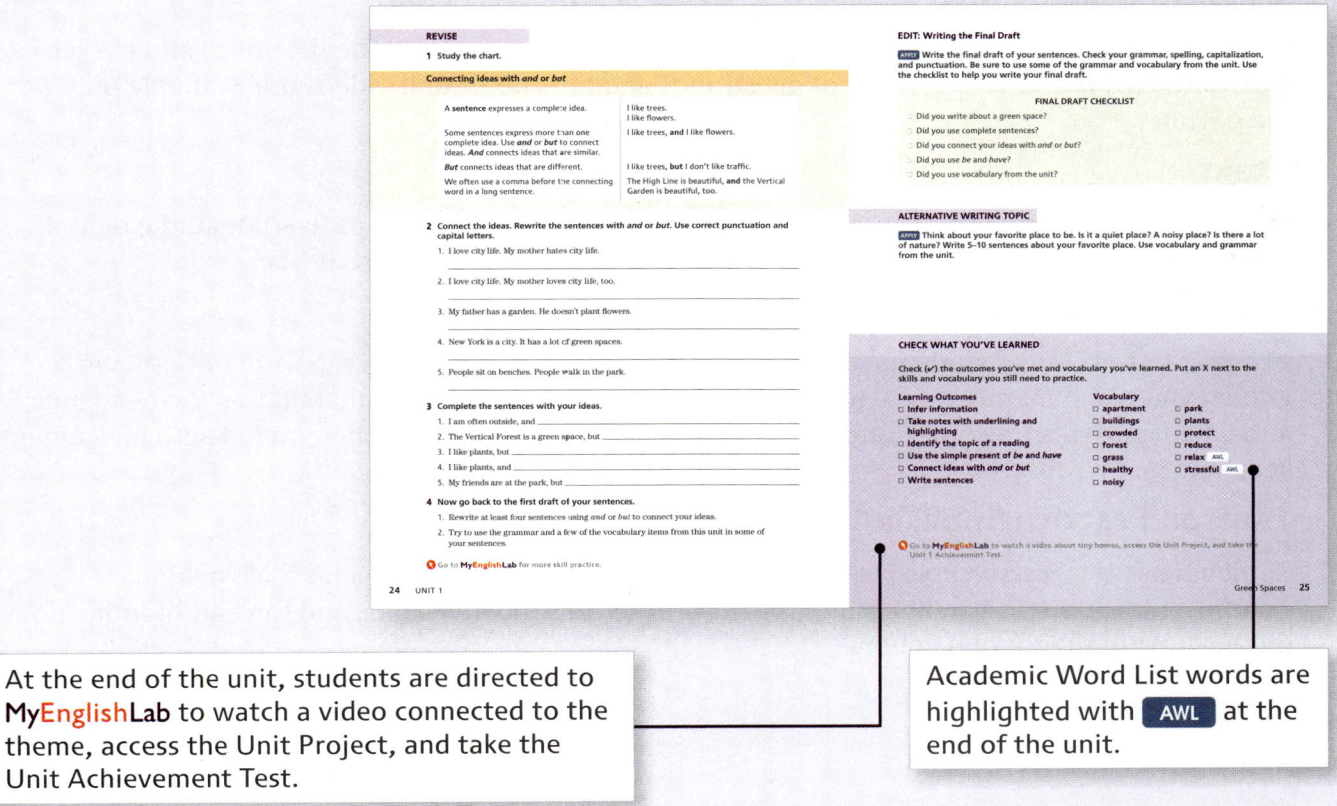

At the end of the unit, students are directed to MyEnglishLab to watch a video connected to the theme, access the Unit Project, and take the Unit Achievement Test.

Academic Word List words are highlighted with AWL at the end of the unit.

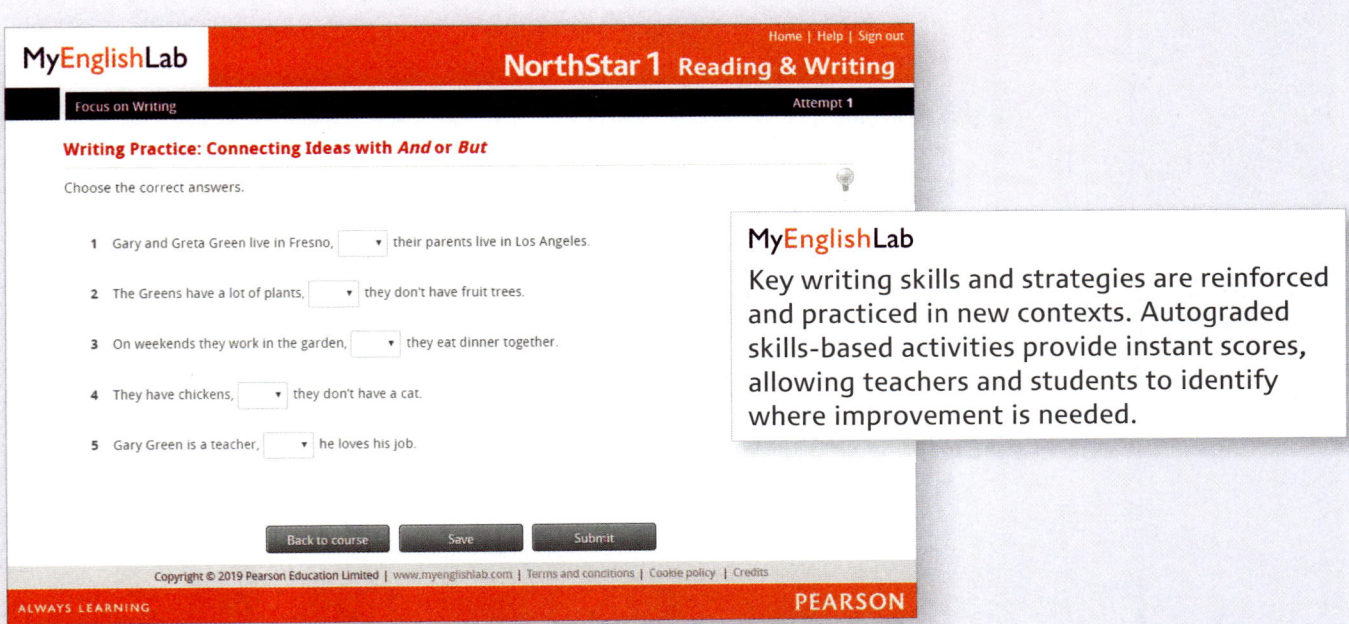

MyEnglishLab
Key writing skills and strategies are reinforced and practiced in new contexts. Autograded skills-based activities provide instant scores, allowing teachers and students to identify where improvement is needed.

The NorthStar Unit   **xi**

COMPONENTS

Students can access the following resources on the Pearson English Portal.

- **Classroom Audio and Videos**

  Classroom audio (the readings for the Reading & Writing strand and the listenings and exercises with audio for the Listening & Speaking strand) and the end-of-unit videos are available on the portal.

- **Etext**

  Offering maximum flexibility in order to meet the individual needs of each student, the digital version of the student book can be used across multiple platforms and devices.

- **MyEnglishLab**

  MyEnglishLab offers students access to additional practice online in the form of both auto-graded and teacher-graded activities. Auto-graded activities support and build on the academic and language skills presented and practiced in the student book. Teacher-graded activities include speaking and writing.

- **Pearson Practice English App**

  Students use the **Pearson Practice English App** to access additional grammar and vocabulary practice, the audio for listenings and readings from the student books, and the end-of-unit videos on the go with their mobile phone.

INNOVATIVE TEACHING TOOLS

With instant access to a wide range of online content and diagnostic tools, teachers can customize learning environments to meet the needs of every student. Digital resources, all available on the Pearson English Portal, include **MyEnglishLab** and ExamView.

Using MyEnglishLab, *Northstar* teachers can

Deliver rich online content to engage and motivate students, including

- student audio to support listening and speaking skills, in addition to audio versions of all readings.
- engaging, authentic video clips tied to the unit themes.
- opportunities for written and recorded reactions to be submitted by students.

Use diagnostic reports to

- view student scores by unit, skill, and activity.
- monitor student progress on any activity or test as often as needed.
- analyze class data to determine steps for remediation and support.

Access Teacher Resources, including

- unit teaching notes and answer keys.
- downloadable diagnostic, achievement and placement tests, as well as unit checkpoints.
- printable resources including lesson planners, videoscripts, and video activities.
- classroom audio.

Using ExamView, teachers can customize Achievement Tests by

- reordering test questions.
- editing questions.
- selecting questions from a bank.
- writing their own questions.

SCOPE AND SEQUENCE

	1 Green Spaces Pages: 2–25 Reading 1: Welcome to the High Line Reading 2: Milan's Vertical Forest	**2 Art for Everyone** Pages: 26–49 Reading 1: Art for Everyone Reading 2: Looking at Haring's Art
Inference	Inferring information	Inferring opinions
Note-Taking	Taking notes with underlining and highlighting	Taking notes with numbers
Reading	Identifying the topic of a reading	Reading numbers
Grammar	The simple present of *be* and *have*	The simple past of *be* and *have*
Revise	Connecting ideas with *and* or *but*	Using commas
Final Writing Task	Sentences	A biography paragraph
Video	Tiny homes	Art

Assessments	Pre-Unit Diagnostic:
	   Check What You Know
	Checkpoint 1
	Checkpoint 2
	Unit Achievement Test
		Pre-Unit Diagnostic:
		   Check What You Know
		Checkpoint 1
		Checkpoint 2
		Unit Achievement Test

Unit Project	Describe a special place	Write about a piece of Keith Haring's art and present it to the class

3 What's It Worth to You?	4 Open for Business
Pages: 50–69 Reading 1: My Secret Reading 2: Be a Smart Collector	Pages: 70–93 Reading 1: The Debate Space: Mom & Pop Vs. Big Box Reading 2: E-Business MagazineProfiles: Etsy.com
Inferring outcomes	Inferring tone
Listing main ideas in notes	Taking notes on examples
Identifying suggestions	Using context clues to understand word meaning
Simple present	*There is/there are*
Writing supporting sentences	Using adjectives in descriptions
A descriptive paragraph	A descriptive paragraph
A stolen wedding dress	Selling hot dogs

Pre-Unit Diagnostic:
   Check What You Know
Checkpoint 1
Checkpoint 2
Unit Achievement Test
	Pre-Unit Diagnostic:
	   Check What You Know
	Checkpoint 1
	Checkpoint 2
	Unit Achievement Test

Write about an antique or collectible	Write an ad to sell a product or a service

SCOPE AND SEQUENCE

	5 What Are You Afraid Of? Pages: 94–117 Reading 1: Help! I'm scared! Reading 2: Other Phobias	**6 What an Adventure!** Pages: 118–141 Reading 1: Lindbergh Did It! Reading 2: Crash Landing on the Hudson River
Inference	Inferring the author's meaning	Making inferences about people
Note-Taking	Taking notes on definitions	Taking notes with a timeline
Reading	Identifying cause and effect	Separating fact from opinion
Grammar	*Can, may, might,* and *will*	The simple past
Revise	Adding supporting detail	Using time order words
Final Writing Task	Suggestions	A narrative paragraph
Video	Weird phobias	A heroic pilot

Assessments	Pre-Unit Diagnostic:
	   Check What You Know
	Checkpoint 1
	Checkpoint 2
	Unit Achievement Test
		Pre-Unit Diagnostic:
		   Check What You Know
		Checkpoint 1
		Checkpoint 2
		Unit Achievement Test

Unit Project	Write about a phobia	Write about a famous person

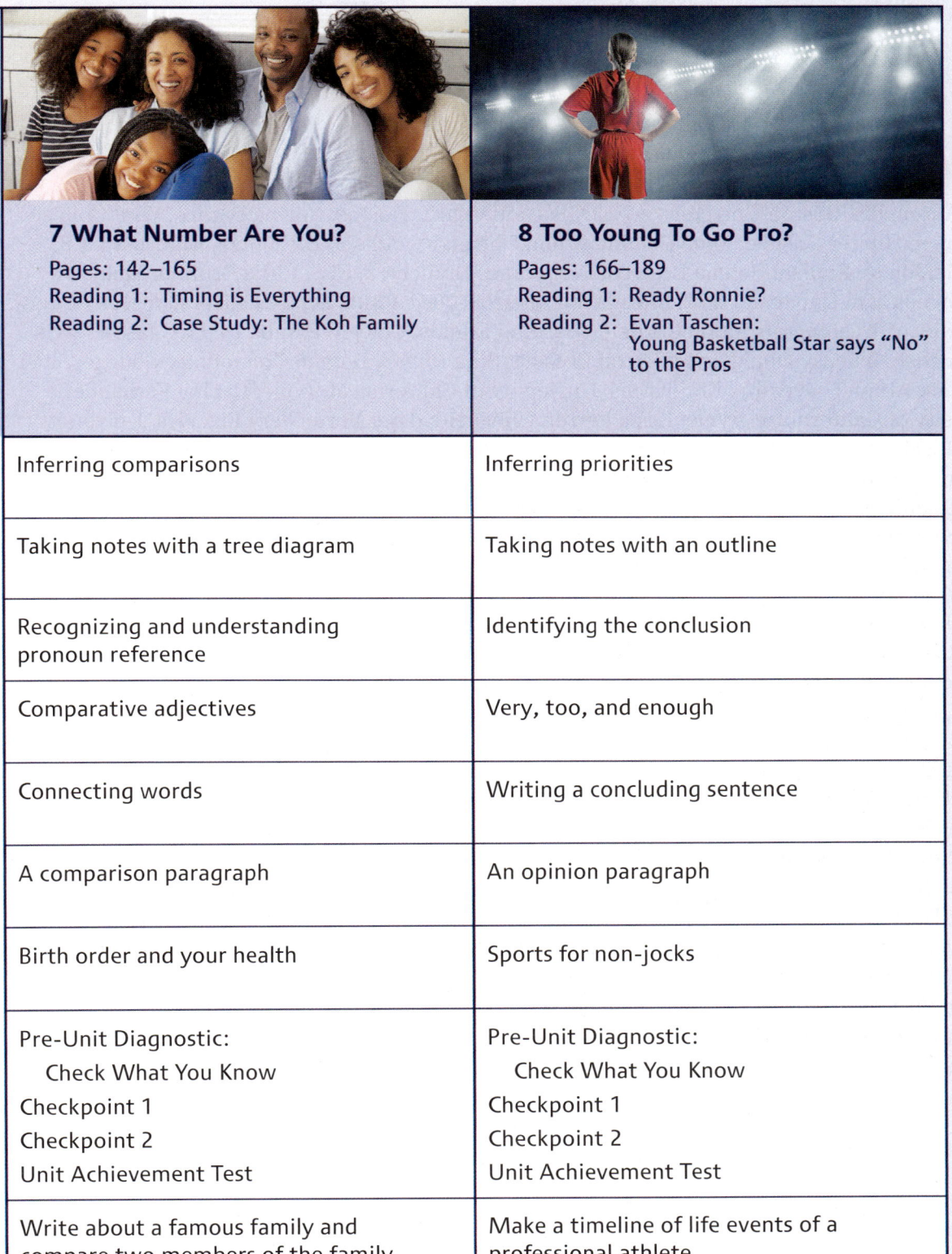

7 What Number Are You?
Pages: 142–165
Reading 1: Timing is Everything
Reading 2: Case Study: The Koh Family

8 Too Young To Go Pro?
Pages: 166–189
Reading 1: Ready Ronnie?
Reading 2: Evan Taschen: Young Basketball Star says "No" to the Pros

Inferring comparisons	Inferring priorities
Taking notes with a tree diagram	Taking notes with an outline
Recognizing and understanding pronoun reference	Identifying the conclusion
Comparative adjectives	Very, too, and enough
Connecting words	Writing a concluding sentence
A comparison paragraph	An opinion paragraph
Birth order and your health	Sports for non-jocks

Pre-Unit Diagnostic:
  Check What You Know
Checkpoint 1
Checkpoint 2
Unit Achievement Test
	Pre-Unit Diagnostic:
	  Check What You Know
	Checkpoint 1
	Checkpoint 2
	Unit Achievement Test

Write about a famous family and compare two members of the family	Make a timeline of life events of a professional athlete

Scope and Sequence   xvii

ACKNOWLEDGMENTS

We would like to offer our sincere thanks to Carol Numrich and Nan Clarke for their insight and guidance.

- John Beaumont and Judith Yancey

REVIEWERS

Chris Antonellis, Boston University – CELOP; Gail August, Hostos; Aegina Barnes, York College; Kim Bayer, Hunter College; Mine Bellikli, Atilim University; Allison Blechman, Embassy CES; Paul Blomquist, Kaplan; Helena Bostros, FLS; James Branchick, FLS; Chris Bruffee, Embassy CES; Joyce Cain, University of California at Fullerton; Nese Cakli, Duzce University; Molly Cheny, University of Washington; María Cordani Tourinho Dantas, Colégio Rainha De Paz; Jason Davis, ASC English; Lindsay Donigan, Fullerton College; Bina Dugan, Bergen Community College; Sibel Ece Izmir, Atilim University; Emily Ellis, University of California at Irvine; Rachel Fernandez, University of California at Irvine; Erica Ferrer, Universidad del Norte; Very Figueira, University of California at Irvine; María Irma Gallegos Peláez, Universidad del Valle de México; Jeff Gano, ASA College; María Genovev a Chávez Bazán, Universidad del Valle de México; Juan Garcia, FLS; Heidi Gramlich, The New England School of English; Phillip Grayson, Kaplan; Rebecca Gross, The New England School of English; Rick Guadiana, FLS; Sebnem Guzel, Tobb University; Esra Hatipoglu, Ufuk University; Brian Henry, FLS; Josephine Horna, Bergen Community College; Judy Hu, University of California at Irvine; Arthur Hui, Fullerton College; Zoe Isaacson, Hunter College; Kathy Johnson, Fullerton College; Marcelo Juica, Urban College of Boston; Tom Justice, North Shore Community College; Lisa Karakas, Berkeley College; Eva Kopernacki, Embassy CES; Drew Larimore, Kaplan, Heidi Lieb, Bergen Community College; Patricia Martins, Ibeu; Cecilia Mora Espejo, Universidad del Valle de México; Oscar Navarro, University of California at Fullerton; Eva Nemtson, ASA College; Kate Nyhan, The New England School of English; Julie Oni, FLS; Willard Osman, The New England School of English; Olga Pagieva, ASA College; Manish Patel, FLS; Paige Poole, Universidad del Norte; Amy Renehan, University of Washington; Claudia Robello, Ibeu; Lourdes Rey, Universidad del Norte; Michelle Reynolds, FLS International Boston Commons; Mary Ritter, NYU; Ellen Rosen, University of California at Fullerton; Dariusz Saczuk, ASA College; Dana Saito-Stehiberger, Univerity of California at Irvine; Miryam Salimov, ASA College; Minerva Santos, Hostos; Sezer Sarioz, Saint Benoit PLS; Gail Schwartz, University of California at Irvine; Ebru Sinar, Tobb University; Beth Soll, NYU (Columbia); Christopher Stobart, Universidad del Norte; Guliz Uludag, UFUK University; Debra Un, NYU; Hilal Unlusu, Saint Benoit PLS; María del Carmen Viruega Trejo, Universidad del Valle de México; Reda Vural, Atilim University; Douglas Waters, Universidad del Norte; Emily Wong, University of California at Irvine; Leyla Yucklik, Duzce University; Jorge Zepeda Porras, Universidad del Valle de México

LEARNING OUTCOMES

- Infer information
- Take notes with underlining and highlighting
- Identify the topic of a reading
- Use the simple present of *be* and *have*
- Connect ideas with *and* or *but*
- Write sentences

Go to **MyEnglishLab** to check what you know.

UNIT 1

Green Spaces

1 FOCUS ON THE TOPIC

1. What do you see in the picture?
2. Where are the people?
3. What are they doing?

2 FOCUS ON READING

READING ONE | Welcome to the High Line

VOCABULARY

1 Look at the picture. Study the words. Then work with a partner. Point to things in the picture that you know.

2 Next, study these words and definitions. Read the words used in sentences.

healthy: not sick, or something that is good for your body or mind
If you eat good food and exercise, you will be **healthy**.

noisy: making a lot of noise (loud sounds)
I live in a city with many people and cars. I don't sleep at night because it is too **noisy**.

stressful: making you worry a lot
Being a parent is **stressful**. Parents worry about their children, work, and homes.

protect: take care of, keep safe, keep away from danger
At the beach, I put on sunscreen. The sunscreen **protects** me from the sun.

reduce: make something smaller or less in size or number
Carbon dioxide (CO_2) is dangerous for people. We need to **reduce** the CO_2 in the air.

relax: become calm, less worried
I like to visit Central Park. At the park, I **relax**. I read a book, listen to music, or sleep.

3 Read the sentences. Then circle the correct word.

1. Hong Kong has a lot of tall (buildings / plants).
2. People walk and play sports in the (plants / park).
3. Mothers and fathers (relax / protect) their children from bad things.
4. Flowers and trees are (buildings / plants).
5. In the city, traffic from the street is (noisy / healthy).
6. Walking to work helps to (protect / reduce) traffic.
7. Fruits and vegetables are (healthy / noisy) for people.
8. Polly is a teacher. Sometimes her work is very (stressful / healthy).
9. Polly works Monday to Friday. She likes to (relax / protect) on Saturdays.
10. The sign says: "Keep off the (buildings / grass)!" We have to walk on the street.

Go to the **Pearson Practice English App** or **MyEnglishLab** for more vocabulary practice.

PREVIEW

You are going to read about a green space. A green space is an area in a city that has grass, trees, flowers, and other plants. A city park is one example of a green space.

Before you read, look at the picture. Compare it to the picture on page 4. Check (✓) your ideas. Then read "Welcome to the High Line."

On page 4, I see . . .

__ trees __ birds
__ flowers __ people
__ plants __ other: _____

In this picture, I see . . .

__ trees __ birds
__ flowers __ people
__ plants __ other: _____

Green Spaces 5

READ

Read this information about the High Line. Create a chart like the one below to take notes. On the left, put the main ideas. On the right, put the details.

TAKE NOTES

Main Ideas	Details
The Highline is a green space	in New York City
	plants/trees/flowers

Go to **MyEnglishLab** to view example notes.

Welcome to the High Line

The High Line is a green space in New York City. The High Line is a good example of using something old in a new way. It is also an example of how green spaces help cities.

Starting in 1934, the High Line was an elevated train line.[1] But in 1980, the High Line closed. For almost twenty years, no one used the High Line. **Plants**, trees, and flowers grew[2] on the train line. In the 1990s, people wanted to take down the High Line because it was very old.

But, in 1999, Joshua David and Robert Hammond started a group: Friends of the High Line. They wanted to **protect** the old train line and make it something new. After ten long years, the High Line opened as a **park** in 2009.

Today, the High Line is a beautiful green space above 10th Avenue. It is 1.45 miles (2.33 km) long. It has more than 350 kinds of plants, trees, and flowers. Some plants are from New York, and other plants are from outside New York.

About 7 million people visit the High Line every year. Visitors have fun with friends and family. They walk around the park, and they look at the plants and the tall **buildings** in New York City. They also sit on benches[3] or on the **grass** and they **relax**. The High Line has music, art, tours, exercise classes, and more. People can learn about plants and **healthy** living. It's all free!

Green spaces like the High Line are good for cities, and they are good for people, too. Today, more than 50% of the world's people live in cities. City life is difficult. It is **noisy**, dirty, and **stressful**. But green spaces **reduce** noise, and they clean the air. They also reduce people's stress. Cities need more green spaces.

At the High Line, what's old is new … and it is better than ever!

For more information about the High Line, go to www.thehighline.org.

[1] **elevated train line:** train tracks that go above the city streets, not on the streets
[2] **grew (verb):** grew is the past form of grow (get bigger in size)
[3] **benches (noun):** places for people to sit in a park

MAIN IDEAS

Choose the correct answer to complete each sentence. Use your notes to help you.

1. In the past, the Highline was _____ .
2. Now, the Highline is _____ .
3. The Highline is in _____ .
4. People need green spaces _____ .

a. a city park
b. to reduce stress
c. New York
d. an elevated train line

DETAILS

1 Complete the sentences with the correct numbers from the reading.

1. The High Line is on _____ th Avenue in New York City.
2. The elevated train line closed in _____ .
3. The Friends of the High Line started in _____ .
4. Today, the High Line park is _____ long.
5. More than _____ kinds of plants, flowers, and trees live in the High Line.
6. _____ people visit the High Line every year.

2 Look at your notes and at your answers in the Preview section. How did your notes help you understand this information?

Green Spaces 7

MAKE INFERENCES 🔍

Inferring Information

An **inference** is an **educated guess** about something. The information is **not stated directly** in the reading.

When you read, some information is easy to find. You can find the information directly in the text. Look at the example:

Is this sentence true or false?

The High Line is a green space in London.

This is false. Paragraph 1 says, "The High Line is a green space in New York City."
But some information is not written directly in the text. You have to *infer*. When you infer, you make a guess (an inference) about the information. Read and use what you know from personal experience. Then put the information together. Look at the example:

Is this sentence true or false?

Joshua David and Robert Hammond care about the High Line.

This is true. The answer is not directly in the text. The text does not say, "They care about the High Line." But we know they care. How? First, we read that Joshua and Robert started the Friends of the High Line (paragraph 3). Second, we read that the Friends of the High Line wanted to protect the High Line (paragraph 3). Third, we know that people protect things because they care about them (personal experience). After reading the text and thinking about what we know, we infer that Joshua and Robert care about the High Line.

Look at Reading One again. Then read each sentence. Write *T* (true) or *F* (false). Look at the paragraphs in parentheses to help you find the answers. Then share your answers with a partner. Point to the sentences in the reading that helped you find the answers.

_____ 1. There is only one kind of green space in cities. (paragraph 1)

_____ 2. All people care about old things. (paragraph 2)

_____ 3. The Friends of the Highline did a lot of hard work to open the park. (paragraph 3)

_____ 4. Today, people are interested in seeing the High Line. (paragraph 5)

_____ 5. The highline is a stressful place. (paragraph 5)

_____ 6. Green spaces can help to make people healthy. (paragraph 6)

DISCUSS

Check (✓) your ideas. Then share your ideas with the class.

Some people like the High Line because _____ .

_____ they like green spaces.

_____ they like walking.

_____ they like birds.

_____ other: _____

> **USE YOUR NOTES**
>
> Use your notes to support your answers with information from the reading.

Some people don't like the High Line because _____ .

_____ they don't like cities.

_____ they don't like walking.

_____ they don't like insects.

_____ other: _____

Cities _____ more green spaces.

_____ need

_____ don't need

▶ Go to **MyEnglishLab** to give your opinion about another question.

READING TWO | Milan's Vertical Forest

PREVIEW

1 Look at the title of Reading Two and the picture. Check (✓) the ideas that you think will be in the reading.

____ benches
____ buildings
____ homes
____ birds
____ insects
____ people
____ gardens
____ green space
____ Other: _____

2 Look at the boldfaced words in the reading. Which words do you already know? What does each word mean?

READ

1 Read the information about Milan's Vertical Forest. Remember to take notes on main ideas and details.

MILAN'S VERTICAL FOREST

Beautiful! The Vertical[1] **Forest** is two tall buildings in Milan, Italy. Inside, the buildings have **apartments** for people to live in. Outside, the buildings are a green space. Plants and trees are on all sides of the buildings. With all these plants, there is less noise from the city. They keep the apartments cool in the summer and warm in the winter.

More important, the trees and plants clean the air. They make oxygen (O_2). That helps the people of Milan to breathe. Also, the Vertical Forest is beautiful for people to look at.

Cities like Milan are very **crowded**. They don't have a lot of space for green spaces. The Vertical Forest has about 800 trees and 11,000 other plants. But it does not use a lot of space.

It's an interesting building! If you go to Milan, be sure to visit the Vertical Forest!

[1] **vertical:** pointing straight up at 90°
vertical ↑ not vertical →

2 Compare your notes on main ideas and details with a partner's. How can you improve your notes next time?

Go to the **Pearson Practice English App** or **MyEnglishLab** for more vocabulary practice.

NOTE-TAKING SKILL

Taking Notes with Underlining and Highlighting

When you read, **underline or highlight** (with a highlighter pen) the most important words and ideas. Look for the names of important people, places, things, or ideas. Underlining or highlighting them will help you **to remember the most important parts** of the reading.

Follow these steps:

1. Read the paragraph or text.
2. Choose the writer's most important words or ideas.
3. Underline or highlight the important words.

Look at this example:

> The <u>High Line</u> is a <u>park</u> on 10th Avenue in <u>New York City</u>. It is a <u>new</u> kind of park. It is an example of how to use an old space in a new way. In the past, the High Line was an <u>elevated train line</u>. Today, the High Line is a beautiful <u>green space</u>.

Your choices might be different. But the writer of this paragraph probably wants the reader to remember these things: the name (the High Line), it is a park, it is different or new, it is in New York City, it was an elevated train line, and today it is a green space. Underlining or highlighting these words and ideas will help you to remember the reading when you review.

Remember: Not every word or idea is important. Do not underline or highlight everything.

1 Read the paragraph. Then underline or highlight the most important words and ideas.

> Green spaces like the High Line are good for cities, and they are good for people, too. Today, more than 50% of the world's people live in cities. City life is difficult. It is noisy, dirty, and stressful. But green spaces reduce noise, and they clean the air. They also reduce people's stress. Cities need more green spaces.

2 Look at Reading Two again. Follow the steps to underline or highlight the most important words and ideas. Compare your answers with a partner.

Go to **MyEnglishLab** for more note-taking practice.

COMPREHENSION

1 Read the sentences. Write *T* (true) or *F* (false).

_____ 1. The Vertical Forest is a park in Milan, Italy.

_____ 2. Inside, the buildings are a green space.

_____ 3. People live inside the buildings.

(continued on next page)

_____ 4. Birds and insects live in the plants.

_____ 5. Plants keep the buildings cool in winter.

_____ 6. Trees and plants clean the air in Milan.

2 Review the boldfaced words from the reading with a partner. Use a dictionary or ask your teacher for any meanings you still do not know.

READING SKILL

1 Look at Reading Two again. Answer the question in two words only.

What is the reading mostly about? _____

Identify the Topic of a Reading

The **topic** of a reading is the general idea of **what the reading is about**. The topic is often stated directly in the title or at the beginning of a reading. Other sentences in the reading say more about the topic.

Example

In Reading Two, the topic is the Vertical Forest. It is mentioned at the beginning of the paragraph. Other sentences in Reading Two describe the Vertical Forest in detail. They answer questions such as *Where is it? What does it have? What does it do? Why is it special or interesting?*

2 Read each paragraph and circle the topic.

> Green spaces are important in cities. People in cities want to see trees, plants, and flowers. They see these things in green spaces. Some examples of green spaces are parks and gardens.

> In the past, the Promenade Plantée was an elevated train line in Paris, France. Today, it is a beautiful green park. The park opened in 1993. That was 16 years before the High Line park in New York City! The Promenade Plantée was the world's first park on an elevated train line. It is very special.

3 Look at Reading One again on page 6. Answer the questions.

What is the topic of the reading? Answer the question in two words only.

_____

How do you know? Point to where the topic is mentioned in Reading One.

🔆 Go to **MyEnglishLab** for more skill practice.

CONNECT THE READINGS

ORGANIZE

The chart compares the High Line in Reading One (R1) with the Vertical Forest in Reading Two (R2). How are the High Line and the Vertical Forest similar? How are they different? Check (✓) Yes or No.

> **USE YOUR NOTES**
>
> Use your notes from Reading One and the information from Reading Two to complete the chart.

	The High Line (R1)		The Vertical Forest (R2)	
	YES	NO	YES	NO
It is a green space.				
It is in a city.				
It is a park.				
It uses an old space in a new way.				
People visit there.				
People live there.				
It has trees, flowers, and other plants.				
It has music and art shows.				
It cleans the air.				
It reduces noise.				

SYNTHESIZE

Answer the questions. Use information from the chart in the Organize section and your own ideas. Write your answers on the lines. Then discuss your answers with a partner.

1. How are the High Line and the Vertical Forest similar?

   _____
   _____

2. How are the High Line and the Vertical Forest different?

   _____
   _____

▶ Go to **MyEnglishLab** to check what you learned.

3 FOCUS ON WRITING

VOCABULARY

REVIEW

Read the postcard. Then complete the message by unscrambling the words in parentheses.

Dear Mom: Hello from New York! I like this city, but life is _____ here. New York is very _____ with people.
1. (flerstuss)   2. (drewcod)

The traffic is very _____. New York has a lot of tall
3. (soniy)

_____, too. But New York also has beautiful green
4. (libgundis)

spaces! Today I visited a _____ called the High Line. I
5. (karp)

can see the High Line from the window of my _____. In
6. (trapmaten)

the past, the High Line was an elevated train line. Now, the

High Line has more than 350 kinds of _____, trees, and
7. (stlapn)

flowers. It's like a _____ inside the city. The plants and
8. (trosef)

trees _____ noise and stress. It is _____ for people
9. (rucdee)   10. (theylah)

here. I love to sit on the _____, read a book, and
11. (srags)

_____. The High Line is a special place. It _____
12. (xelar)   13. (poetctrs)

nature in the city. You will love it! I miss you!

Visit soon! — Terry

Fiona Rouse
144 Main Street,
Apt. #4C
Phoenix, AZ 85051

EXPAND

Study the chart. Pay attention to the boldfaced words.

A *noun* is a person, place, or thing. a person a place a thing	friend, Robert Hammond park, New York City buildings
Most *verbs* show action. Some verbs do not show an action.	live, walk, protect, relax be (am, is, are), seem, feel
Sometimes a noun and a verb can have the same word form.	They have a beautiful **garden**. (noun) They **garden** on weekends. (verb) My sister gave me a green **plant** for my apartment. I **plant** flowers in my garden. I go for a **walk** in the park on Sundays. I **walk** in the park.

To understand the difference, begin by asking:
    Is it a person, place, or thing?
    Is it an action?
 	
                      Nouns:
                      Verbs:
	
	The Vertical Forest has a lot of **plants** and **trees**.
	My friend **loves** flowers.
	She **plants** flowers outside her house.

Read the sentences. Fill in the blanks with words from the box. Then check (✓) *noun* or *verb*.

| garden | plants | visit | walk |

1. a. My family is in Milan, so I _____ Milan often.

   ___ noun   ___ verb

   b. When I plan a _____ to Milan, I will see the Vertical Forest.

   ___ noun   ___ verb

2. a. I have a nice _____ . It has beautiful flowers and plants.

   ___ noun   ___ verb

   b. I _____ often. I love growing things and being outside.

   ___ noun   ___ verb

3. a. People _____ in the park and sit on benches.

   ___ noun   ___ verb

   b. Some people take a _____ outside every day.

   ___ noun   ___ verb

4. a. Green spaces have _____ such as flowers and trees.

   ___ noun   ___ verb

   b. My friend _____ flowers in his garden.

   ___ noun   ___ verb

CREATE

APPLY Write three more sentences about the High Line or the Vertical Forest. Use one word from the Review or Expand section in each sentence.

Example

People visit the High Line every year.

1. _____
2. _____
3. _____

 Go to the **Pearson Practice English App** or **MyEnglishLab** for more vocabulary practice.

GRAMMAR FOR WRITING

1 Read the passage. Underline forms of the verbs *be* and *have*.

> The High Line is a green space in New York City. It isn't a building, and it doesn't have apartments. It has flowers, plants, and trees. Two men in New York City made the High Line. Their names are Joshua David and Robert Hammond.

SIMPLE PRESENT: BE

The present of the verb **be** has three forms: *am, is,* and *are.* 1. Use *am, is,* or *are* to make an **affirmative statement**.	**I am** from London. **You are** from Beijing. **She is** from Milan. **He is** from Milan. **It is** a park. **We are** happy in nature. **They are** friends.
2. Use *am, is,* or *are* + *not* to make a **negative statement**.	**I am not** from Chicago. **You are not** from Shanghai. **She / He is not** from Auckland. **It is not** a building. **They are not** sad.
3. We often use **contractions** (short forms) in speaking and informal writing. **NOTE:** There are two negative contractions for *is not* and *are not*.	**I'm** from London. **You're** from Beijing. **She's / He's** from Milan. **It's** a park. **I'm not** from Chicago. **You're not** from Shanghai. / You **aren't** from Shanghai. **She's / He's not** from Auckland. She / He **isn't** from Auckland. **It's not** a park. / It **isn't** a park.
4. Use *be* to talk about **measurements** and **age**.	The High Line **is** 1.45 miles **long**. It **is** more than 10 years **old**. NOT: The High Line ~~has~~ 1.45 miles. It ~~has~~ more than 10 years old.

Green Spaces

SIMPLE PRESENT: *HAVE*

The present of the verb **have** has two forms: *have* and *has*.

1. Use *have* or *has* to make an **affirmative statement**.

   I **have** a beautiful garden.
   You **have** a nice apartment.
   He **has** a beautiful garden.
   She **has** a beautiful garden.
   It **has** flowers, plants, and trees.
   We **have** green spaces.
   They **have** trees.

2. Use *do not have* or *does not have* to make a **negative statement**.

   I **do not have** a garden.
   We **do not have** a garden.
   You **do not have** a garden.
   He **does not have** an apartment.
   It **does not have** apartments.

3. We often use **contractions** (short forms) in speaking and informal writing.

   I **don't have** a garden.
   You **don't have** a garden.
   He **doesn't have** an apartment.
   It **doesn't have** apartments.
   We **don't have** a garden.
   They **don't have** a garden.

2 Look at the picture. Then complete the passage. Use correct forms of *be* (*am, are, is, am not, are not, is not*) or *have* (*have, has, don't have, doesn't have*).

Our Community¹ Garden

Our community garden _____1._____ a green space in our neighborhood. All the people in my building take care of the garden. It _____2._____ 70 feet (21.3m) long and 25 feet (7.62m) wide. It _____3._____ big like a park, but it _____4._____ a lot of plants. When people visit, they _____5._____ surprised. They say, "Wow! You _____6._____ a lot of plants in that small space!" We grow a lot of vegetables for eating. Vegetables _____7._____ healthy. Also, we grow ten kinds of flowers: roses, daisies, and more. The flowers _____8._____ beautiful. Our community garden _____9._____ trees. Our community garden _____10._____ fun. It _____11._____ a special place for me.

_____

¹ **community** (noun): all the people living in one place

UNIT 1

3 **Write sentences about the Vertical Forest.**

1. The Vertical Forest / be / a green space
   The Vertical Forest is a green space.

2. It / be / in Milan, Italy

3. It / not be / a park

4. The Vertical Forest / have / apartments inside

5. It / have / trees and plants outside

6. I / be / interested in visiting the Vertical Forest

7. The Vertical Forest and the High Line / be / green spaces

8. The Vertical Garden / have / less noise from the city

9. I / be / interested in living in the Vertical Forest

10. My city / not have / a park like the Vertical Forest

11. I / not have / an apartment in the Vertical Forest

12. Green spaces / be / important

4 APPLY **Look at the picture. Write sentences about the green space. Use** *be* **or** *have*. **Then compare your sentences with a partner.**

Example

The park **has** trees. It **does not have** a vegetable garden.

1. _____
2. _____
3. _____
4. _____
5. _____

Go to the **Pearson Practice English App** or **MyEnglishLab** for more grammar practice. Check what you learned in **MyEnglishLab**.

FINAL WRITING TASK: Sentences   APPLY

In this unit, you read about two different green spaces: the High Line and the Vertical Forest.

Now you are going to *write sentences about a green space you know.* Use the vocabulary and grammar from the unit.

For an alternative writing topic, see page 25.

PREPARE TO WRITE: Categorize Information

Think about a green space you know. Remember that a lot of places are green spaces: a park, a forest, a garden, a yard, a building, even a store or a café. A green space can be in your city, in a city you visited, or on TV.

To help you plan your sentences, you are going to **categorize information** about your green space: ***things you see*** there and ***things you do*** there.

Study the chart. Then make your own chart below.

The High Line

Things you see	Things you do
1.45 miles of park	walk
city streets (below)	sit on benches
gardens	look at plants
plants	look at buildings
trees	relax
grass	learn about plants and healthy living
people / visitors / tourists	exercise
benches	
buildings	
art	

Your green space: _____

Things you see	Things you do

WRITE: A sentence

The Sentence

1. A sentence is a group of words that expresses a complete idea. A sentence can make a statement or ask a question.

2. A sentence has a subject and a verb. **BUT:** In commands, don't use a subject (*you*).	[subject] [verb] The High Line is a new kind of park. [subject] [verb] People look at plants. [subject][verb] My friends love to visit green spaces. [verb] Meet me at the High Line.
3. The first word in a sentence begins with a capital letter.	The High Line is a place to walk, sit, and enjoy nature. Green spaces are important.
4. Use a **period** at the end of a sentence. Use a **question mark** at the end of a question. Use an **exclamation point** at the end of a sentence with strong feeling. Do not leave a space before the **punctuation** at the end of a sentence.	The High Line has many plants, trees, and flowers**.** Is it a building**?** Wow! The High Line is beautiful**!** **Correct:** Do you like the High Line? I love it. **Not Correct:** Do you like the High Line ? I love it .

1 Rewrite the sentences. Add capital letters and punctuation (a period, a question mark, or an exclamation point) as needed.

1. what is Seoullo 7017
2. seoullo 7017 is in Seoul, South Korea
3. it is an elevated green space
4. it opened in 2017
5. it is a lot of fun
6. visitors look out over the city
7. seoullo 7017 has more than 24,000 plants
8. it has blue lights at night
9. are you interested in Seoullo 7017
10. visit Seoullo 7017

2 Look at each group of words. If it is a complete idea with correct grammar, punctuation and capitalization, check (✓) *sentence*. If not, check *not a sentence*, and change it to make it correct.

	sentence	not a sentence
1. My green space ^is the High Line.		✓
2. Hyde Park is in London.	✓	
3. The Vertical Forest in Milan.		
4. Is a beautiful building.		
5. My friend lives in the Vertical Forest		
6. It have plants?		
7. My green space is my garden.		
8. My garden very beautiful.		
9. We have fun at the park.		
10. we like watching birds		

3 **APPLY** Write 10 sentences about a green space. These sentences are your first draft. Your first draft is the first time you write your ideas. Your first draft is different from your final draft. You will make some changes later. Use the information on page 21. Begin like this:

My green space is . . . or *The name of my green space is . . .*

1. _____
2. _____
3. _____
4. _____
5. _____
6. _____
7. _____
8. _____
9. _____
10. _____

REVISE

1 Study the chart.

Connecting ideas with *and* or *but*

A **sentence** expresses a complete idea.	I like trees. I like flowers.
Some sentences express more than one complete idea. Use **and** or **but** to connect ideas. **And** connects ideas that are similar.	I like trees, **and** I like flowers.
But connects ideas that are different.	I like trees, **but** I don't like traffic.
We often use a comma before the connecting word in a long sentence.	The High Line is beautiful, **and** the Vertical Garden is beautiful, too.

2 Connect the ideas. Rewrite the sentences with *and* or *but*. Use correct punctuation and capital letters.

  1. I love city life. My mother hates city life.
     _____

  2. I love city life. My mother loves city life, too.
     _____

  3. My father has a garden. He doesn't plant flowers.
     _____

  4. New York is a city. It has a lot of green spaces.
     _____

  5. People sit on benches. People walk in the park.
     _____

3 Complete the sentences with your ideas.

  1. I am often outside, and _____
  2. The Vertical Forest is a green space, but _____
  3. I like plants, but _____
  4. I like plants, and _____
  5. My friends are at the park, but _____

4 Now go back to the first draft of your sentences.

  1. Rewrite at least four sentences using *and* or *but* to connect your ideas.
  2. Try to use the grammar and a few of the vocabulary items from this unit in some of your sentences.

Go to **MyEnglishLab** for more skill practice.

EDIT: Writing the Final Draft

APPLY Write the final draft of your sentences. Check your grammar, spelling, capitalization, and punctuation. Be sure to use some of the grammar and vocabulary from the unit. Use the checklist to help you write your final draft.

> **FINAL DRAFT CHECKLIST**
> ☐ Did you write about a green space?
> ☐ Did you use complete sentences?
> ☐ Did you connect your ideas with *and* or *but*?
> ☐ Did you use *be* and *have*?
> ☐ Did you use vocabulary from the unit?

ALTERNATIVE WRITING TOPIC

APPLY Think about your favorite place to be. Is it a quiet place? A noisy place? Is there a lot of nature? Write 5–10 sentences about your favorite place. Use vocabulary and grammar from the unit.

CHECK WHAT YOU'VE LEARNED

Check (✔) the outcomes you've met and vocabulary you've learned. Put an X next to the skills and vocabulary you still need to practice.

Learning Outcomes
☐ Infer information
☐ Take notes with underlining and highlighting
☐ Identify the topic of a reading
☐ Use the simple present of *be* and *have*
☐ Connect ideas with *and* or *but*
☐ Write sentences

Vocabulary
☐ apartment
☐ buildings
☐ crowded
☐ forest
☐ grass
☐ healthy
☐ noisy
☐ park
☐ plants
☐ protect
☐ reduce
☐ relax [AWL]
☐ stressful [AWL]

Go to **MyEnglishLab** to watch a video about tiny homes, access the Unit Project, and take the Unit 1 Achievement Test.

LEARNING OUTCOMES

> Infer opinions
> Take notes with numbers
> Read numbers

> Use the simple past of *be* and *have*
> Use commas
> Write a biography paragraph

Go to My**English**Lab to check what you know.

UNIT 2

Art for Everyone

1 FOCUS ON THE TOPIC

1. Look at the picture. What is this person doing?
2. Is this art? Why or why not?

2 FOCUS ON READING

READING ONE | Art for Everyone

VOCABULARY

1 Read the words and their definitions.

ad: short for *advertisement*; words or pictures that make you want to buy something

energetic: very active

famous: known by a lot of people

museum: a place to look at (not buy) art

drawing: a picture made with a pencil, pen, or chalk[1]

painting: a picture made with paint

sculpture: art made with wood, stone, or metal

public: for everyone to see or use

graffiti: pictures and writing made on public walls and buildings

---

[1] **chalk:** Teachers use chalk to write on the board.

an ad

a drawing

a painting

28 UNIT 2

2 Keith Haring was an American artist who lived from 1958 to 1990. Complete each sentence with one of the words. You may need to use the plural form.

1. Keith Haring liked to work and play a lot. He was very _____energetic_____ .
2. The artists Picasso and Michelangelo are more _____ than Keith Haring.
3. Today, people can see Haring's art in _____ in Brazil, Europe, Japan, and the United States.
4. Haring also made _____ to sell things in magazines.
5. In the early 1980s, Haring made his art in a lot of _____ places in New York. He wanted everyone to see his art.
6. When he made a _____ , Haring used different colored pens, pencils, and chalk.
7. Haring put _____ on the walls of buildings and in the subway in New York City.
8. Leonardo da Vinci's *Mona Lisa* is a _____ .
9. Michelangelo's *David* is a very well-known _____ .

Go to the **Pearson Practice English App** or **MyEnglishLab** for more vocabulary practice.

a sculpture

graffiti

Art for Everyone

PREVIEW

You are going to read a magazine interview. Before you read the interview, look at the timeline about Keith Haring's life. Then complete the chart.

May 4, 1958	Haring is born in Kutztown, Pennsylvania.
1978	Haring goes to New York City. He studies at the School of Visual Arts. He draws graffiti in the NYC subway.
1979	Haring leaves the School of Visual Arts.
1981	The NYC police arrest[1] him for drawing in the subway.
1982	He stops making graffiti. He has his first art show at the Tony Shafrazi Gallery in NYC.
1983–1987	Haring works in Asia, Europe, and the USA.
1986	He paints a picture on the Berlin Wall in Germany. He opens the Pop Shop in NYC to sell his art.
1988	He opens the Pop Shop in Tokyo, Japan.
1989	Haring starts The Keith Haring Foundation to help children and people with AIDS.
February 16, 1990	He dies of AIDS.

What people, places, things, and ideas / activities were important to Keith Haring? Complete the chart.

People	Places	Things	Ideas / Activities
			art

READ

Read the interview. Create a chart like the one below to take notes. On the left, put the main ideas. On the right, put the details.

TAKE NOTES

Main Ideas	Details
Keith Haring was an artist.	graffiti, drawings, paintings, sculptures
His art is about social issues.	

Go to **MyEnglishLab** to view example notes.

---

[1] **arrest:** take (someone) to jail

Read the interview. *Art World Magazine* (AW) talked to Edwin Ramon (ER) about Keith Haring. Mr. Ramon is a DJ and an independent art curator in New York and Los Angeles.

Art for Everyone

Untitled, 1984

Radiant Baby

1 **AW:** Mr. Ramon, what kind of person was Keith Haring?

2 **ER:** Haring liked people. He liked parties and dancing. He was **energetic**. You can see his energy in his art. His art moves and dances, too.

3 **AW:** When did Haring become **famous**?

4 **ER:** In 1978, he started to make pictures in the New York City subway. Some people were very upset. They said, "This isn't art. It's **graffiti!**"

5 But graffiti is art. And some people like his art very much. They started to buy his **drawings**, **paintings**, and **sculptures**. Then galleries[1] became interested in his art, too. By the end of the mid-1980s, Keith Haring was famous around the world.

6 **AW:** What is Haring's art about? What does it mean?

7 **ER:** When people asked Haring, "What is your art about?" he answered, "You decide." His art is funny, energetic, and sometimes angry. It is also political.[2]

8 His art is about education, freedom, and AIDS. These three social issues were very important to Haring. His art is about children, too. He worked with kids on many projects. For example, in the late 1980s, he made a large sculpture for a children's hospital in New York.

9 **AW:** Was Haring different from other artists?

10 **ER:** Yes, he was.

11 **AW:** How was he different?

12 **ER:** He was different in two ways. First, Haring liked to make art in **public** places, like in the subway. He believed "art is for everyone." In the early 1980s, he was famous for his public art. Later, he became famous in galleries and **museums**.

13 Second, he was different because magazines had **ads** with his drawings and paintings in them. People also bought his art at the two Pop Shops. At the Pop Shop, there were T-shirts, watches, and buttons with his art. Nothing was very expensive.

14 **AW:** Is his art still popular?

15 **ER:** Yes, it is. Haring died on February 16, 1990, but people still feel his energy in his art. Today, we can see his art all around the world. Some of the money from his art helps AIDS organizations and children's organizations. His art still helps people. And if people want to learn more, they can go to www.haring.com.

16 **AW:** Interesting. Thank you very much, Mr. Ramon.

17 **ER:** It was my pleasure.

---

[1] **galleries:** places to look at and buy art. A gallery is also a room inside a museum.

[2] **political:** relating to politics or government of a country

MAIN IDEAS

Read each sentence. Circle the correct answer to complete the sentence. Use your notes to help you.

1. In the early 1980s, Haring's art was in the _____ of New York City.

    a. hospitals

    b. museums

    c. subways

2. Haring's art was about _____ .

    a. social issues

    b. his family

    c. famous people

DETAILS

1 Complete the sentences with the words from the box. Use each word only once.

| ads | decide | energy | graffiti | money | public | social issues |

1. You can see his _____ in his art.

2. Some people said his work was just _____ and not really art.

3. First, he was famous for his _____ art.

4. He made _____ for magazines.

5. People asked, "What is your art about?" Haring answered, "You _____ ."

6. _____ , like AIDS and freedom, were important to Haring.

7. Some of the _____ from the Pop Shop helped AIDS organizations and children's organizations.

2 Look back at your notes and your answers for Main Ideas and Details. How did your notes help you complete the exercises?

MAKE INFERENCES

Inferring Opinions

An **inference** is an **educated guess** about something. The information is **not stated directly** in the reading. Good readers put ideas together to find the right answer. Direct questions about main ideas and details are often easy to answer. Inference is more difficult. Writers do not always state an opinion directly. You need to use what you know and information in the text to infer a writer's opinion.

Look at the example. Answer the question and read the explanation:

Do you think making money was important to Haring? Check (✓) your answer.

☐ Yes

☐ No

In paragraph 2, we learn that he made art in the subway but not for money.

In paragraph 8, we learn that he sold his art at the Pop Shop but for low prices.

After reading closely, we infer that making money was not very important to Haring.

1 According to the interview, why did Keith Haring make art? Check (✓) the best answer. Look at the paragraphs in parentheses.

Keith Haring used his art to _____ . (paragraphs 4, 5, 6, and 7)

☐ help his family

☐ communicate with people

☐ make a lot of money for himself

☐ pay for his art school education

2 Now discuss your answers with a partner. Point out the sentences in the paragraphs that helped you find the answer.

DISCUSS

Complete the sentences. Then share your ideas with the class.

Some people like Keith Haring's art because it is

_____ .

Some people don't like Keith Haring's art because it is

_____ .

> **USE YOUR NOTES**
>
> Use your notes to support your answers with information from the reading.

▶ Go to **MyEnglishLab** to give your opinion about another question.

READING TWO | Looking at Haring's Art

PREVIEW

1. Look at the pictures and the title of Reading Two. Check (✓) the ideas that you think will be in the reading.

   ☐ AIDS

   ☐ Animals

   ☐ Art

   ☐ Money

   ☐ Travel

   ☐ Other: _____

2. Look at the boldfaced words in the reading. Which words do you already know? What does each one mean?

READ

1. Read the paragraph about Keith Haring's art. Remember to take notes on main ideas and details.

LOOKING AT HARING'S ART

Some of Keith Haring's art was just for fun. Other pieces were about social or **political** issues. Here are two examples. First, in 1985, Haring made 20,000 *Free South Africa* **posters**— pictures or drawings made on strong paper and put on city walls. He wanted people to work together for freedom in that country. Second, Haring made *Stop AIDS*. That was in 1989. The snake is a symbol, or image, of AIDS. The scissors are people working together to stop AIDS.

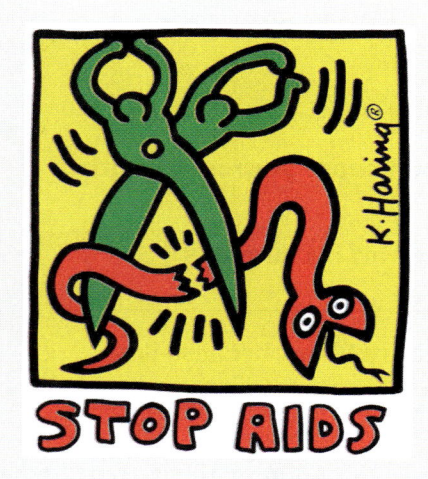

2. Compare your notes on main ideas and details with a partner. How can you improve your notes next time?

Go to the **Pearson Practice English App** or **MyEnglishLab** for more vocabulary practice.

NOTE-TAKING SKILL

The Short and Long Forms of Numbers

When you take notes, use the short form of numbers. The short form will help you to write faster.

Cardinal Numbers		Ordinal Numbers	
long	**short**	**long**	**short**
zero	0	—	—
one	1	first	1st
two	2	second	2nd
three	3	third	3rd
four, five, six, seven, eight, nine, ten	4, 5, 6, 7, 8, 9, 10	fourth, fifth, sixth, seventh, eighth, ninth, tenth	4th, 5th, 6th, 7th, 8th, 9th, 10th
eleven, twelve, thirteen . . .	11, 12, 13 . . .	eleventh, twelfth, thirteenth . . .	11th, 12th, 13th . . .
twenty	20	twentieth	20th
twenty-five	25	twenty-fifth	25th
thirty	30	thirtieth	30th
one hundred	100	one hundredth	100th
three thousand thirty-three	3033	three thousand thirty-third	3033rd

For more about cardinal and ordinal numbers, see page 37.

Here are two other ways to shorten numbers:

When you write the number for a year (for example, 1958), you can use the short form ('58) if you know the year and can remember it.

          long   **short**
Haring was born in 1958. = *Haring was born in '58.* (1958, not 1858)

To shorten a number in the thousands that ends in 000 (2,000), you can shorten it by replacing the 000 with the letter K (2K).

    One thousand = 1,000 = 1K
    Three hundred fifty thousand = 350,000 = 350K
    Three hundred fifty thousand and one = 350,001 (You cannot use K.)

When you take notes, the short form of numbers is OK. But in academic writing (sentences and paragraphs), write the numbers 0–9 in long form (*zero, one, two, three,* etc.). Use the short form for 10 and over (*10, 11, 12, 13, 500,* etc.) in academic writing.

    Your notes: *Haring's sister → 5 paintings, 25 drawings*
    Academic sentence: *Haring's sister has five paintings and 25 drawings.*

1 **Write the numbers in short form.**

Eighty thousand: _____

Fifteen: _____

Seventeen seventy-six: _____

Sixty-sixth: _____

Two hundred thousand: _____

The year you were born: _____

2 **Look at Reading Two again. In your notebook, write the long and short form of each number in Reading Two.**

COMPREHENSION

1 **Each sentence is false (not true). Change the underlined word to make it true.**

1. All of Keith Haring's art was just for fun.

2. The scissors in *Stop AIDS* symbolize "AIDS."

3. Haring made 20,000 paintings for people in South Africa in 1985.

2 **Review the boldfaced words from the reading with a partner. Use a dictionary or ask your teacher for any meanings you still do not know.**

READING SKILL

1 **Look at Reading Two again. Look at the numbers. What information do the numbers give? Complete the chart to put the numbers in groups: order (first, second, third . . .), quantity (how many: 1, 2, 3 . . .), or date.**

Order	Quantity	Date
	Two	

Identifying Important Numbers

When you read, notice important numbers. Numbers will help you understand the reading.

- Ordinal numbers show order: *first (1st), second (2nd), third (3rd), fourth (4th), fifth (5th)*
- Cardinal numbers show quantity, or "how many": *one (1), two (2), three (3)*
- Dates (Years): *1964, 2015*

    1964 = "nineteen sixty-four"
    2020 = "twenty twenty"
    December 3, 1932 = "December third, nineteen thirty-two"

    Note that the number for the "day" (3) is written as a cardinal number, but you say it as an ordinal number (third).

2 Look at the timeline on page 30 and Reading One on page 31. Underline the numbers. Then find two examples of numbers for order, quantity, or date. Write the sentences from the text.

Order

1. First, Haring liked to make art in public places, like in the subway.
2. _____

Quantity

1. _____
2. _____

Date

1. _____
2. _____

Go to **MyEnglishLab** for more skill practice.

CONNECT THE READINGS

ORGANIZE

Look at Haring's pictures again. What important ideas are in Haring's art? Check (✓) the boxes. Then share your answers with the class.

> **USE YOUR NOTES**
>
> Use your notes from Reading One and the information from Reading Two to complete the chart.

Ideas in Haring's Art	Radiant Baby	Untitled, 1984	Free South Africa	Stop AIDS
POLITICS				
AIDS				
LOVE				
ENERGY				
FREEDOM				
CHILDREN				
OTHER: _____				

SYNTHESIZE

Use information from the chart in the Organize section to complete the sentences. Use each item (the names of the pictures and the ideas) only once.

1. _____(picture) is about _____(idea) and the fight for _____(idea) in a country. Haring wanted people to be free.

2. In the 1980s and 1990s, _____(idea) was a serious problem—even more than today. It was a problem for Haring and for everyone. _____(picture) shows that people can work together to end a serious problem.

3. For Haring, _____(idea) were a symbol of hope for the future. _____(picture) shows this idea. In the picture, there are rays around the child—like the rays of the sun. The rays show the _____(idea) of the child.

4. In _____(picture), we see a person. The person's arms go through his heart and brain. In this picture, Haring shows that _____(idea) is difficult sometimes.

🔎 Go to **MyEnglishLab** to check what you learned.

38 UNIT 2

3 FOCUS ON WRITING

VOCABULARY

REVIEW

Complete the crossword puzzle with the words from the box.

ads	drawings	galleries	painter	~~public~~	social
art	energy	graffiti	pop	sculpture	symbol
different	famous	museum	poster	~~shop~~	

Across

1. In 1988, Haring opened the Pop _____ in Tokyo. It closed in 1989.
6. He believed "_____ is for everyone."
8. The word _____ is short for "popular."
9. Some people said, "That is not art. It's just _____."
10. _____ issues were very important to Haring.
11. Haring had a lot of _____ . You can see it in his art. It "moves."
12. The word _____ is short for "advertisements."
13. A wedding ring is a _____ of marriage.
16. A _____ is a work of art made of materials such as metal, stone, or wood.

Down

2. Haring made _____ art. He wanted everyone to see it.
3. People around the world know Haring. He is a _____ artist.
4. Someone who draws makes _____ .
5. Haring was _____ from other artists.
7. A person who paints is a _____ .
9. By the mid-1980s, Haring's work was in many art _____ around the world.
14. *El Prado* is a famous _____ in Madrid, Spain.
15. When I was a teenager, I had a *Happy Baby* _____ on my bedroom wall.

Art for Everyone 39

EXPAND

Study the two charts. The vocabulary from the unit is in bold.

Nouns	Adjectives	Verbs
dance dancer dancing	X	dance
drawing	X	draw
energy	**energetic**	energize
freedom	free	free
paint **painting** painter	X	paint
politics politician	political	X
poster post	posted	post
the public	**public**	publicize
sculpture sculptor sculpting	X	sculpt
symbol (of)	X	symbolize

A **noun** names: a **person** (an artist, Pablo Picasso) a **place** (a museum, London) a **thing** (a drawing) an **idea** (freedom) or **activity** (dancing) Nouns for people end in *-ist, -er, -or,* or *-ian* *Painting* and *drawing* have two meanings. One is a **thing** (count noun) and one is an **activity** (non-count noun). Note: A person who paints is a **painter**, but a person who **draws** is an artist, not a **"drawer."** Note: A singular count noun usually has a word like *a, an,* or *the* before it.	Person: **Pablo Picasso** is a famous **painter.** Place: **London** is a big city. Thing: The *Mona Lisa* is a famous **painting.** Activity: **Painting** is a popular hobby. Her **drawings** are beautiful. She likes **drawing** pictures. **A** baby in Haring's art is **a** symbol of life. **The** man in **the** photo is Andy Warhol.
An **adjective** describes a noun. Some adjectives, like *energetic, artistic,* and *public* end in *-ic*.	a **large** picture a **famous** person a **public** place
Most **verbs** show action. Other verbs like *be, have,* and *like* do not show action.	Sofia **paints** very well. She **draws** well, too. Sofia **is** from Australia. She **has** a sister and a brother. She **likes** to practice yoga.

Complete the sentences with the correct form of the words.

1. (dance / dancing / dancer)

    The tango is a _____ from Argentina.

    Julio Bocca is a famous tango _____ from Argentina.

    Bocca's _____ is beautiful.

2. (draw / drawing)

    This is a good _____ of my father. It looks like him.

    We _____ every day in art class.

    Children enjoy _____ in school.

3. (energetic / energy / energize)

    Patrick is too tired to dance. He has no _____ .

    A cup of coffee will _____ him.

    If he sleeps well tonight, he will be more _____ tomorrow.

4. (free / freedom)

    In this country, people are _____ to say almost anything.

    Not every country has this _____ .

5. (paint / painter / painting)

    I have to buy more _____ at the art store.

    I want to finish this _____ . It's a picture of my house.

    _____ is a fun activity.

    I'm a good _____ .

6. (political / politics / politicians)

    I am not interested in _____ .

    My teacher's ideas are very _____ .

    Many _____ are honest, but some are not.

7. (post / posts / posters)

    My sister has five _____ of her favorite movie actor on her bedroom wall.

    My friends _____ photos of their vacations on Facebook®.

    I like to read the _____ on your blog. You are a good writer.

8. (public / the public / publicize)

    _____ likes the new show at the Shafrazi Gallery very much.

    They _____ the big art shows on TV and in newspapers.

    Mila likes to go to _____ places like parks and shopping malls.

Art for Everyone

9. (sculptor / sculpture / sculpting)

   Constantin Brancusi is a famous _____ .

   The Kiss is a _____ by Brancusi.

   _____ was one way he made art.

10. (symbol / symbolizes)

    The color red _____ both "stop" and "love."

    A red ribbon is a _____ of AIDS awareness.

CREATE

APPLY Write three more sentences about Keith Haring and his art. Use one word from the chart on page 40 in each sentence.

1. _____
2. _____
3. _____

Go to the **Pearson Practice English App** or **MyEnglishLab** for more vocabulary practice.

GRAMMAR FOR WRITING

1 Read the information about Keith Haring. Then answer the questions.

AW: Was Haring different from other artists?

ER: Yes, he was.

AW: How was he different?

ER: Haring liked to make art in public places, like in the subway. He believed "art is for everyone." First, he was famous for his public art. Later, he became famous in galleries and museums. He was also different because magazines had ads with his paintings and drawings. His drawings were also on other things, such as Swatch watches. He also sold his art in the Pop Shop. He used his art in unusual ways to communicate with the world.

2 Underline *was, were,* and *had* in the interview on the previous page. How many examples can you find?

was _____   were _____   had _____

When do we use *am, is, are,* and *have*?
☐ present   ☐ past

When do we use *was, were,* and *had*?
☐ present   ☐ past

The Simple Past of *Be*

1. The simple past forms of *be* are *was* and *were*.	Keith Haring **was** an artist. Social issues **were** important to him.
2. For negative sentences use: subject + *was / were* + *not* Use the long form in formal writing. In speaking and informal writing, use *wasn't / weren't*.	 His art **was not** in museums in the early 1980s. His parents **were not** famous. His art **wasn't** in museums in the early 1980s. His parents **weren't** famous.
3. For *yes / no* questions, use: *was / were* + subject	 **Was Haring** different from other artists? Yes, he was. **Were his drawings** popular? Yes, they were. **Was Haring** famous in the 1970s? No, he wasn't.
4. For *Wh-* questions, use: *Wh-* word + *was / were* + subject	 **Who was** Keith Haring? **What was** his art about? **How were** his pictures different?

The Simple Past of *Have*

1. The simple past form of *have* is *had*.	Haring **had** a lot of energy.
2. For negative sentences, use: *did* + *not* + *have*	Haring **did not have** a brother.
In speaking and informal writing, use: *didn't have*	Haring **didn't have** a brother.
3. For *yes / no* questions, use: *did* + subject + *have*	**Did** Haring **have** fun with his art? Yes, he did. **Did** Haring **have** a long career? No, he didn't.
4. For *Wh-* questions, use: *Wh-* word + *did* + subject + *have*	**Where did** Haring **have** fun? **When did** Haring **have** the most success?

3 Complete each sentence with *was, wasn't, were, weren't, had,* or *didn't have*.

1. Keith Haring and Andy Warhol _____were_____ famous artists in the 1980s.
2. Both Haring and Warhol _____ from Pennsylvania, but they _____ from different cities.
3. Haring and Warhol (not) _____ the same age. Warhol _____ 31 years older than Haring.
4. Warhol and Haring _____ a lot of friends.
5. Warhol _____ a student at the Carnegie Institute of Technology.
6. In the 1950s, Warhol _____ a job on Madison Avenue in New York.
7. He _____ an artist for *Vogue* and *Glamour* magazines.
8. He (not) _____ a lot of money at that time.
9. By the early 1960s, Andy Warhol _____ a famous Pop artist.
10. Like Haring's art, Warhol's art _____ controversial.
11. Warhol _____ a painter, sculptor, writer, and filmmaker.
12. Keith Haring _____ a painter and a sculptor, but he (not) _____ a writer or a filmmaker.
13. Warhol and Haring _____ good friends in the 1980s.
14. Haring _____ very sad when Warhol died in 1987.
15. Warhol _____ 58 years old when he died.
16. He (not) _____ a very long life.

4 **Work with a partner. Write questions about Keith Haring and his art. Use the past forms of *be* and *have*.**

1. Who / be / Keith Haring?

    Who was Keith Haring?

2. Be / Haring / famous in the 1970s?

3. Be / Keith Haring / energetic?

4. In what city / be / Haring / born?

5. Be / Haring / only a painter?

6. Why / be / his art / controversial?

7. Be / the Pop Shop / a restaurant?

8. Where / be / the two Pop Shops?

9. How old / be / Keith Haring / in 1990?

5 APPLY **Give your book to your partner. Your partner will write answers to your questions in full sentences.**

Your partner's answers:

1. *Keith Haring was an artist in the 1980s.*
2.
3.
4.
5.
6.
7.
8.
9.

Go to the **Pearson Practice English App** or **MyEnglishLab** for more grammar practice. Check what you learned in **MyEnglishLab**.

Art for Everyone

FINAL WRITING TASK: A Biography Paragraph APPLY

In this unit, you read a timeline and an interview about Keith Haring. You also looked at examples of Keith Haring's art.

You are going to **write a biography paragraph about Keith Haring.** A biography is a story of a person's life. Use the grammar and vocabulary from the unit.

For an alternative writing topic, see page 49.

PREPARE TO WRITE: Finding Information in a Reading

To help you plan your biography, you are going to **look for information in the readings** as a prewriting activity.

1 Look at the timeline on page 30. Then answer the questions about Keith Haring.

1. Where was Keith Haring born?
   <u>Keith Haring was born in Kutztown, Pennsylvania.</u>

2. When was Keith Haring born?
   _____

3. When was Haring arrested by the police? Why was he arrested?
   _____

4. When and where was Haring an art student?
   _____

5. What were his first drawings? Where were they?
   _____

6. When and where was Haring's first important art show?
   _____

2 Look at Reading One on page 31. Find one more idea about Keith Haring that you think is interesting. Write it on the line. Use this information in your biography, too.

_____

WRITE: Time Order

A biography usually gives events in **time order** (in the order they happened). The writer begins with the first event and ends with the last event.

1 Read the sentences about Andy Warhol. Number the sentences in time order from 1 to 7.

_____ a. Warhol was a student at Carnegie Institute of Technology from 1945 to 1949.

_____ b. Andy Warhol and Keith Haring were good friends in the 1980s.

_____ c. Andy Warhol died in 1987.

_____ d. By the early 1960s, Andy Warhol was a famous Pop artist.

__1__ e. Andy Warhol was born in Pennsylvania in 1928.

_____ f. In the 1950s, Warhol was a commercial artist on Madison Avenue in New York.

_____ g. Then Warhol had his first art show in 1952.

2 Work with a partner. Compare your answers for Exercise 1. Were your answers the same as your partner's? Talk about any differences.

3 Look at your answers to the questions about Keith Haring in Prepare to Write on page 46. Put them in time order.

4 Write your first draft. Include a topic sentence that gives the main idea of your paragraph. Write sentences to explain or support the main idea. Don't worry about grammar yet. Just try to make your ideas clear.

---

[1] **commercial artist:** an artist who works for an advertising company

REVISE: Using Commas

Using commas correctly makes your writing clearer and easier to understand.

1 Study the chart.

Using Commas

Use commas:	
• in complete dates between the day and the year.	Keith Haring was born on May 4, 1958.
• between a city and country or state.	The Harings were from Kutztown, Pennsylvania. Haring visited Madrid, Spain.
• after the city *and* country (or state) *when* there are more words after the country / state.	They lived in Kutztown, Pennsylvania, in the 1970s. Haring visited Madrid, Spain, many times.
Do not use commas:	
• if the month and year are separated by a preposition.	Haring was born in May **of** 1958.
• if the city and country (or state) names are separated by more information.	Kutztown **is in the state of** Pennsylvania.
• if the city, state, country, name of the month, or year is used alone.	The Harings were from Kutztown. Haring lived in Pennsylvania when he was young. Haring visited Spain many times. Haring was born in May. He was born in 1958.

2 Add commas to these sentences. Not every sentence needs commas.

1. Haring was born on May 4 1958.
2. Haring moved to New York New York in 1978.
3. He had his first important show in 1982.
4. Haring opened The Pop Shop in New York City in 1986. It closed in September of 1995.
5. The Pop Shop in Tokyo Japan opened on January 30 1988. It closed in 1989.
6. Haring died on Friday February 16 1990.

3 APPLY Write three sentences about yourself (for example, your address or your birthday). Use commas correctly.

1. _____
2. _____
3. _____

4 Now go back to the first draft of your paragraph.

a. Rewrite at least three to four sentences using the simple past of *be* and *have*.

b. Try to use the grammar, commas, and a few of the vocabulary items from this unit in some of your sentences.

 Go to **MyEnglishLab** for more skill practice.

EDIT: Writing the Final Draft

APPLY Write the final draft of your paragraph. Check your grammar, spelling, capitalization, and punctuation. Be sure to use some of the grammar and vocabulary from the unit. Use the checklist to help you write your final draft.

FINAL DRAFT CHECKLIST

- ☐ Did you use a capital letter at the beginning of each sentence?
- ☐ Did you use a period at the end of each sentence?
- ☐ Did you use the past forms of *be* and *have*?
- ☐ Did you use commas in the correct places?
- ☐ Did you use vocabulary from the unit?
- ☐ Did you put the events in time order?

ALTERNATIVE WRITING TOPIC

APPLY Look at the pictures on page 38 again. Choose one picture. What do you see? What is it about? How does it make you feel? Write five to ten sentences about this picture. Use the vocabulary and grammar from the unit.

CHECK WHAT YOU'VE LEARNED

Check (✔) the outcomes you've met and vocabulary you've learned. Put an X next to the skills and vocabulary you still need to practice.

Learning Outcomes
- ☐ Infer opinions
- ☐ Take notes with numbers
- ☐ Read numbers
- ☐ Use the simple past of *be* and *have*
- ☐ Use commas
- ☐ Write a biography paragraph

Vocabulary
- ☐ ad
- ☐ dance, dancer, dancing
- ☐ draw, drawing
- ☐ energy, energetic, energize **AWL**
- ☐ famous
- ☐ free, freedom
- ☐ graffiti
- ☐ museum
- ☐ paint, painting, painter
- ☐ politics, politician, political
- ☐ post, poster, posted
- ☐ public, the public, publicize
- ☐ sculpt, sculpture, sculptor, sculpting
- ☐ symbol, symbolize **AWL**

 Go to **MyEnglishLab** to watch a video about art, access the Unit Project, and take the Unit 2 Achievement Test.

LEARNING OUTCOMES

- Infer outcomes
- List main ideas in notes
- Identify suggestions
- Use simple present

- Write a topic sentence
- Write supporting sentences
- Write a descriptive paragraph

Go to **MyEnglishLab** to check what you know.

UNIT 3

What's It Worth to You?

1 FOCUS ON THE TOPIC

1. What are some things that people collect?
2. Why do people have collections?

2 FOCUS ON READING

READING ONE | My Secret

VOCABULARY

Read the passage. Then write the boldfaced word next to its definition. Compare your answers with a partner's.

ANTIQUES ROADSHOW

Antiques Roadshow is a popular television show. The show travels to different cities. The **guests** are regular people. They bring their special possessions to the show. They tell stories and ask questions.

The guests bring many kinds of **items**. Some guests bring antiques. Antiques are old and sometimes **valuable** things, such as art, furniture, or jewelry. Other guests bring **collections** of many toys or books. Some items are very common and are not **worth** a lot of money. But others are very valuable. Some of the items are in very bad **condition**, but others are in great condition—just like new. Some items have only **sentimental** value—maybe the item was a gift from someone special or brings back good memories. Maybe it is just an item the guest likes a lot—a **favorite** item.

Antiques **experts** give information about the items. The experts also say how much the items are worth. The guests always want to know the value of their items.

People can learn a lot on this show. This type of TV show started in England more than 20 years ago. You can see shows like it in other countries around the world.

_____ 1. people with a lot of knowledge and experience with something

_____ 2. people who visit a person or place

_____ 3. having a value in personal feelings or emotions

_____ 4. objects or things

_____ 5. the physical state of something—good or bad

_____ 6. having a high price; worth a lot of money

_____ 7. groups of things that people like to keep

_____ 8. equal to, in money

_____ 9. being liked more than others

Go to the **Pearson Practice English App** or **MyEnglishLab** for more vocabulary practice.

PREVIEW

Dan Stone writes a sports column for the *Boston Daily News*. Read the first part of an article about Dan Stone. Then, with a partner, guess: What is Dan Stone's secret[1]?

MY SECRET
by Dan Stone

I am a sports writer, and I love my job because I love sports. But I have a little secret.

Every Monday night I watch my favorite TV show. If the telephone rings, I don't answer it. I tell my friends that I am watching *Monday Night Football*, but that isn't true.

Now read Dan Stone's column on the next page.

READ

Read the sports column. Create a chart like the one below to take notes. On the left, put the main ideas. On the right, put the details.

TAKE NOTES

Main Ideas	Details
Antiques Roadshow:	TV show about antiques and …
Dan Stone:	

Go to **MyEnglishLab** to view example notes.

---

[1] **secret:** information that you don't tell other people

MY SECRET
by Dan Stone

1. I am a sports writer, and I love my job because I love sports. But I have a little secret.

2. Every Monday night I watch my **favorite** TV show. If the telephone rings, I don't answer it. I tell my friends that I am watching *Monday Night Football*, but that isn't true.

3. Sometimes my favorite show is more exciting than *Monday Night Football*. Here is my secret: On Monday nights I watch *Antiques Roadshow*. It is a show about antiques and **collections**. Fourteen million people watch it every week.

4. The show is simple. The **guests** on the show are real people. The guests bring in old art, furniture, books, toys, and more. First, the guests tell the **experts** about their items. Then the experts talk about the **items**. Finally, the experts say how much the items are **worth**. You get a lot of information.

5. One woman, Veronica, had an old painting. Veronica's grandmother got the picture for free in 1925. The expert looked at Veronica's picture carefully and said, "Thomas Cole is the artist. Cole painted this around 1835. Your painting is worth about $125,000." Veronica was very surprised. She told the expert, "Wow! That's a lot of money! But I don't care about the money. The painting has a lot of **sentimental** value."

6. I want *Antiques Roadshow* to visit my city. I can't wait! I have a baseball signed by Babe Ruth and Jackie Robinson in the 1940s. It's in perfect **condition**. I also have a baseball card collection. I keep it in a box under my bed. The ball and the cards have sentimental value.

7. My father gave them to me. But I don't really like to play or watch baseball. Maybe they're worth a lot of money!

8. And you? Are you ready? Look carefully around your home! You might have something very **valuable**.

MAIN IDEAS

Read each sentence. Check (✓) True or False. Then write the number of the paragraph where you found the answer.

	True	False	Paragraph Number
1. People who watch *Antiques Roadshow* can learn a lot.	☐	☐	_____
2. Dan Stone watches football on Monday nights.	☐	☐	_____
3. *Antiques Roadshow* is a sports show.	☐	☐	_____
4. *Antiques Roadshow* buys items from the guests.	☐	☐	_____

DETAILS

1 Match each question to the correct answer. Then write the number of the paragraph where you found the answer.

__c__ 1. What do Stone's friends think he watches on Monday nights? __2__

_____ 2. How many people watch *Antiques Roadshow* every week? _____

_____ 3. What do people bring to *Antiques Roadshow*? _____

_____ 4. How much is the woman's painting worth? _____

_____ 5. What items does Stone have from his father? _____

    a. items from home

    b. $125,000

    c. ~~football~~

    d. a signed baseball and his baseball cards

    e. 14 million

2. Look at your notes and at your questions in the Preview section. How did they help you understand the article?

MAKE INFERENCES

Inferring Outcomes

An **inference** is an **educated guess** about something. The information is **not stated directly** in the reading. Good readers put ideas together to find the answer. Writers don't always say what will happen next. A reader can make an inference, or guess the outcome. Inferring an outcome can help you better understand what you read.

Look at the example. Check *probably yes* or *probably no.* Then read the explanation.

Veronica will sell her painting.

_____ probably yes

_____ probably no

The best answer is *probably no.* How do we know?

In paragraph 6, we learn the painting is worth $125,000. Veronica says, "That's a lot of money! But I don't care about the money. The painting has a lot of sentimental value."

We know Veronica does not care about the money. We know the painting has sentimental value. We understand that for Veronica, the money isn't important. After reading closely, we can guess that Veronica will not sell her painting.

1 Read each sentence. Check (✓) *probably yes* or *probably no.* Look at the numbered paragraphs to help you find the answers.

1. Dan's friends will laugh at him if they learn his secret. (paragraph 2)

   _____ probably yes

   _____ probably no

2. Dan will take his signed baseball and his baseball cards to *Antiques Roadshow.* (paragraph 6)

   _____ probably yes

   _____ probably no

3. Dan will sell his signed baseball and his baseball cards. (paragraph 6)

   _____ probably yes

   _____ probably no

2 Share your answers with a partner. Point to sentences that helped you find the answers.

DISCUSS

In his column, Dan Stone said, "Fourteen million people watch it every week." Why is *Antiques Roadshow* popular? Check (✓) all the possible answers. Then share your answers with the class.

> **USE YOUR NOTES**
>
> Use your notes to support your answers with information from the reading.

Antiques Roadshow is popular because _____ .

_____ 1. people like learning

_____ 2. people need money

_____ 3. the people on the show are funny

_____ 4. people remember their family's past

_____ 5. the items are interesting

_____ 6. the guests are real people

_____ 7. your idea: _____ .

▶ Go to **MyEnglishLab** to give your opinion about another question.

READING TWO | Be a Smart Collector

PREVIEW

1 Look at the title of Reading Two and the picture on page 58. What do you think Reading Two will say about smart collectors? Check (✓) your answers.

Smart collectors . . .

_____ collect beautiful items

_____ collect common items

_____ collect items people like

_____ collect items worth a lot of money

_____ other: _____

2 Look at the boldfaced words in the reading. Which words do you already know? What does each one mean?

READ

1 Read the rules from an expert about art collecting. Remember to take notes on main ideas and details.

BE A SMART COLLECTOR

Starting a collection is easy, but be a smart collector. Here are four rules:

RULE 1

Enjoy. Collect things that you are interested in. Collect things that you want to keep for a long time.

RULE 2

Learn. Become an expert. Read a lot. Talk to antiques experts. Ask a lot of questions. Don't worry! Experts love to talk.

RULE 3

Look for the best. Collect things in good condition. For example, an antique toy in "mint," or perfect, condition will be valuable in the future. A **similar** toy in bad condition will not be as valuable.

RULE 4

Collect **rare** items. Rare things are more valuable than common things. If the items you collect are rare today, they will be more valuable in the future.

2 Compare your notes on main ideas and details with a partner's. How can you improve your notes next time?

Go to the **Pearson Practice English App** or **MyEnglishLab** for more vocabulary practice.

NOTE-TAKING SKILL

Listing Main Ideas

In this section, you will focus on listing main ideas. Here are some important definitions:

A **topic** is the general idea that the reading is about.
The **main ideas** are the main points about the topic.
Details explain or support the main ideas.

Read this short paragraph and study the chart.

People collect many things. Some people collect art. Art collectors buy paintings, drawings, and photographs. Other people collect sports items. They collect balls, cards, and clothes from their favorite sport. Some people collect books, too. Old or rare books are valuable.

The **topic** is things people collect.

Main ideas about the topic are:	Details:
Some people collect art.	Art collectors buy paintings, drawings, and photographs.
Other people collect sports items.	They collect balls, cards, and clothes from their favorite sport.
Some people collect books, too.	Old or rare books are valuable.

When you take notes, use bullet points (•) to list the main ideas. Only use key words.

People collect:

- art
- sports items
- books

1 Read about Dan Stone's collection. Write the topic. Then make a list of the three main ideas about this topic. Use three bullet points.

Dan Stone has a collection. He has a baseball signed by Babe Ruth and Jackie Robinson in the 1940s. It's in perfect condition. He also has baseball cards. He keeps the cards in a box under his bed. He has a signed football, too. The football was signed by Joe Montana in the 1980s.

Topic: _____

- _____
- _____
- _____

2 Look at Reading Two again. In your notebook, write the topic. Then make a list of the four main ideas in Reading Two. Use four bullet points.

Go to **MyEnglishLab** for more note-taking practice.

COMPREHENSION

1 Match each example with one of the rules in the reading. Write the rule number (*1, 2, 3,* or *4*) on the line.

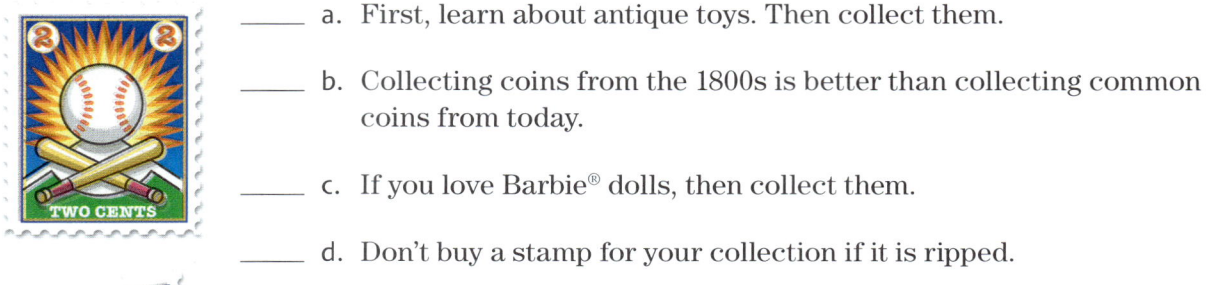

_____ a. First, learn about antique toys. Then collect them.

_____ b. Collecting coins from the 1800s is better than collecting common coins from today.

_____ c. If you love Barbie® dolls, then collect them.

_____ d. Don't buy a stamp for your collection if it is ripped.

A ripped stamp

2 Review the boldfaced words from the reading with a partner. Use a dictionary or ask your teacher for any meanings you still do not know.

READING SKILL

1 Look at Rule 1 from Reading Two again. In Rule 1, the writer wants the reader to do three things. What are they? Underline the writer's three suggestions.

Identifying Suggestions

When you read, it's important to notice when the writer wants you to do something. Writers often use commands, called **imperatives,** to make suggestions.

In Unit 1, you learned that a sentence has a subject and a verb. **Imperatives** are the base form of the verb without a subject. The subject is not written, but we understand that the subject is *you*.

Understood Subject

Subject   Verb
(You)   Enjoy.
(You)   Collect things that you are interested in.
(You)   Collect things that you want to keep for a long time.

These are the writer's three suggestions in Rule 1.

2 Look at Rules 2, 3, and 4 in Reading Two. Underline the suggestions.

Go to **MyEnglishLab** for more skill practice.

60 UNIT 3

CONNECT THE READINGS 🔍

ORGANIZE

Read Dan Stone's column again. How does Dan follow the four rules? Match the ideas about Dan's collection with the rules for collecting on page 58. Write the letter of the idea on the line next to the rule.

> **USE YOUR NOTES**
>
> Use your notes from Reading One and the information from Reading Two to complete the chart.

	Ideas From Dan Stone's Column
RULE 1: ENJOY _____	a. The baseball is rare. It was signed by two famous baseball players.
RULE 2: LEARN _____	b. His baseball is in perfect condition.
RULE 3: LOOK FOR THE BEST _____	c. He watches *Antiques Roadshow*.
RULE 4: COLLECT RARE ITEMS _____	d. Dan doesn't like baseball, but his signed baseball has sentimental value.

SYNTHESIZE

Dan Stone has a collection of baseball items. Is Dan Stone a smart collector? Did he follow the four rules? Complete the first sentence. Then write four or five more sentences to explain.

Dan Stone (is / isn't) a smart collector. He _____

_____

_____

_____

_____

▶ Go to **MyEnglishLab** to check what you learned.

3 FOCUS ON WRITING

VOCABULARY

REVIEW

Complete the sentences with the correct words.

1. (condition / valuable)

    I found some of my childhood toys in my mother's house. Maybe they are _____ today. They are all in good _____ .

2. (guest / worth)

    My mother wants to be a _____ on *Antiques Roadshow*. She wants to bring her antique watch. The watch isn't _____ very much, but she enjoys wearing it.

3. (collection / favorite)

    I love art. My _____ artist is Claude Monet. A museum in Paris has a big _____ of Monet's paintings.

4. (sentimental / rare / similar)

    This was my grandparents' kitchen table. It is very _____ , so you can't buy a _____ table today. It isn't a beautiful table, but I keep it because it has a lot of _____ value.

5. (expert / items)

    My father likes to read about the past. He is an _____ on the U.S. Civil War. He knows a lot about it, and he collects _____ from the war.

62 UNIT 3

EXPAND

Remember that a **noun** names a person, place, thing, or idea. An **adjective** is a word that describes a noun. A **verb** is a word that shows an action.

Many nouns end in *-tion*, *-ment*, *-ity*, and *-or*. Many adjectives end in *-ing*, *-ed*, *-al*, *-able*, and *-ible*.

Many words such as *expert* and *sports* are both a noun and an adjective.

Work with a partner. In your notebook, make a chart like the one below. Put the words into the correct group.

collect	collector	excited	~~expert~~	similar	valuable
collectible	condition	excitement	possession	similarity	value
collection	excite	exciting	sentimental	sports	

Nouns	Adjectives	Verbs
expert	expert	

CREATE

APPLY Write your special possession or collection on the first line. Then write sentences about it. Use one word from the Expand or Review section in each sentence.

Example
My special possession is a watch. It is valuable.

1. _____
2. _____
3. _____
4. _____

Go to the **Pearson Practice English App** or **MyEnglishLab** for more vocabulary practice.

GRAMMAR FOR WRITING

1 Read the excerpt from "My Secret." Then answer the questions.

> I am a sports writer, and I love my job because I love sports. But I have a little secret.
>
> Every Monday night I watch my favorite TV show. If the telephone rings, I don't answer it. I tell my friends that I am watching *Monday Night Football,* but that isn't true.

1. How many verbs are there? Underline them.
2. Which verbs are negative? Circle them.
3. What are these sentences about? Circle a, b, or c.

   a. the past   b. the present   c. the future

The Simple Present

1. Use the **simple present** for everyday actions or facts.	I **have** a secret. On Monday nights, I watch *Antiques Roadshow*. If the telephone **rings,** I **don't answer** it.
2. When the subject is *he*, *she*, or *it*, put an **-s** at the end of the regular verbs. REMEMBER: *be* and *have* are irregular.	She collect**s** antique jewelry. *Antiques Roadshow* **is** my favorite show. Dan **has** a secret.
3. For negative sentences, use: ***do / does*** + ***not*** + **the base form of the verb** Use the contractions ***don't*** and ***doesn't*** in speaking and informal writing.	Dan **does not watch** football on Mondays. I **do not like** to play golf. If the telephone rings, I **don't** answer it.
4. For ***yes / no* questions**, use: ***Do / Does*** + **subject** + **the base form of the verb** Use ***do*** or ***does*** in short answers.	**Do diamonds cost** a lot? Yes, they **do**. **Does Dan Stone watch** football on Mondays? No, he **doesn't**.
5. For ***wh-* questions**, use: ***Wh-*** word + ***do / does*** + **subject** + **the base form of the verb**	**What do you watch** on Monday nights? **Where do you like** to play golf? **How much does that car cost?**

2 Complete the conversation with the simple present form of each verb.

EXPERT: Welcome to *Antiques Roadshow*. What ____*do*____ you ____*have*____ with
                                                         1. (have)
you today?

WOMAN: I _____ my mother's diamond wedding ring. I love this ring! I _____
            2. (have)   3. (remember)
my mother when I _____ it.
                   4. (wear)

EXPERT: _____ you _____ it often?
                        5. (wear)

WOMAN: Yes, I _____ . I never _____ it off.
                  6. (do)   7. (take)

EXPERT: What _____ you _____ about this ring?
                              8. (know)

WOMAN: My father gave it to my mother in 1964. I _____ where he got it.
                                                    9. (not / know)
My husband _____ that it _____ worth a lot of money.
            10. (not / think)   11. (be)
_____ it _____ valuable to you?
               12. (look)

64   UNIT 3

EXPERT: Well, it _____ a beautiful ring, but I have some bad news. This _____
          13. (be)   14. (not / be)
a real diamond. It _____ fake. It is worth about $50.
                    15. (be)

WOMAN: Really? My husband was right! Well, I still _____ it. My husband and I
                                                       16. (love)

_____ to give it to our daughter. She _____ the ring, too.
17. (plan)   18. (love)

3 **APPLY** Work with a partner. Write three questions to ask your partner about a special item in his or her family, or about a favorite item. Use *yes / no* and *wh-* questions.

1. _____
2. _____
3. _____

Exchange books and answer each other's questions. Use simple present verbs.

1. _____
2. _____
3. _____

Go to the **Pearson Practice English App** or **MyEnglishLab** for more grammar practice. Check what you learned in **MyEnglishLab**.

FINAL WRITING TASK: A Paragraph **APPLY**

In this unit, you read about special possessions and collections. Now you are going to **write a paragraph about your own special possession or collection.** Use the vocabulary and grammar from the unit.

For an alternative writing topic, see page 69.

PREPARE TO WRITE: Asking Yourself Questions

To get ideas for your writing, you are going to **ask yourself questions** about a topic. Asking yourself questions helps you to think about the topic and connect to it. For example: *Do I have a special possession or collection? What is it? Why do I keep it? Was it a gift? Does it have sentimental value? Is it worth a lot of money*?

1 Think of some special possessions or collections that you have. Make a list of four or five items. A special possession can be something that:

- you collect.
- you received as a gift.
- helps you remember a special person, event, or time in your life.

Example

My Special Possessions:

my high school soccer shirt   my grandfather's painting   family photos

2 Choose two special possessions from the list you made. Ask yourself the questions and write short answers in the chart. You can add questions of your own.

	Possession 1	Possession 2
1. What is my special possession?		
2. Where did I get it?		
3. How much is it worth?		
4. Why do I keep it?		
5.		
6.		

3 Choose one possession to write about.

WRITE: A Paragraph

Remember that a **paragraph** is a group of sentences about one main idea on the topic. The first sentence usually gives the main idea of the paragraph. This sentence is the topic sentence. The other sentences explain or support the topic sentence.

1 Read the paragraph. Then answer the questions.

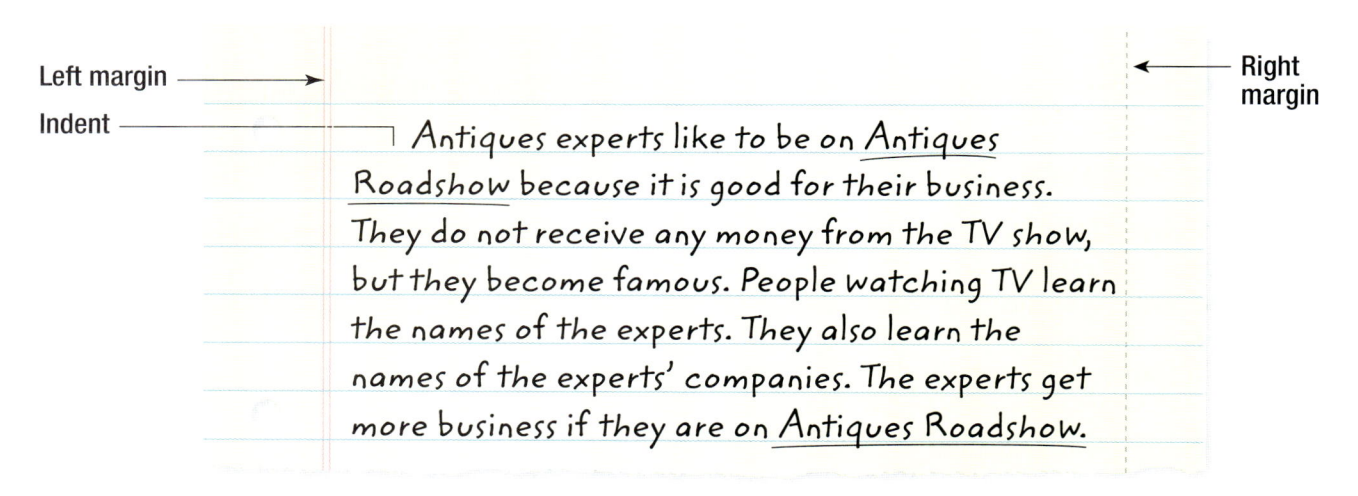

Left margin →
Indent →

Antiques experts like to be on Antiques Roadshow because it is good for their business. They do not receive any money from the TV show, but they become famous. People watching TV learn the names of the experts. They also learn the names of the experts' companies. The experts get more business if they are on Antiques Roadshow.

← Right margin

1. What is the main idea of this paragraph? Circle the sentence that has the main idea.
2. Does the writer begin each new sentence on a new line, or does the writer continue on the same line?
3. When does the writer stop and move down to the next line?

2 Write two paragraphs with these sentences on a separate piece of paper. The sentences are in the correct order. Follow the rules for paragraph form. Your paragraphs will look like the paragraph in Exercise 1.

Then work with a partner and compare your papers. Do your paragraphs look the same? Do they look like the model?

Sentences for Paragraph 1

One day, a man named Russ Pritchard was a guest on *Antiques Roadshow*.

He had a large sword.

When he was young, Pritchard found the sword in his new house.

George Juno, an antiques expert, told Pritchard it was an American Civil War sword.

Juno said the sword was very rare and worth $35,000.

Pritchard was very surprised to hear this.

Sentences for Paragraph 2

Two years later, there was a story in the newspaper about Pritchard and Juno.

WGBH, a Boston TV station, learned that Pritchard's story was not true.

Pritchard and Juno made up the story together.

WGBH was very angry because it wants only true stories on *Antiques Roadshow*.

As a result, Juno cannot be on *Antiques Roadshow* in the future.

3 Read the paragraph. Underline the topic sentence.

One of my special possessions is my collection of family photographs. I have hundreds of photos. I have very old photos of my great-grandparents. I also have pictures of my grandparents' wedding. I especially love the photos of my parents when they were children. Sometimes I spend hours looking at the pictures. I like the photos because my family is very important to me.

4 Read the paragraph. It is missing a topic sentence. Read the topic sentences. Choose the best topic sentence and write it on the line.

_____. It is yellow and black and has the number "11" on it. It also has my name on the back. I got it in high school when I played on the school's team. Our team won every game. The shirt has a lot of sentimental value. I keep it because I like to remember those games and my teammates. We had a lot of fun together.

Topic Sentences

a. My team won every game in high school.

b. My high school soccer shirt is very important to me.

c. Soccer is my favorite sport.

What's It Worth to You?

5 Look back at Prepare to Write, Exercise 3, on page 66. What special possession are you going to write about? Write a topic sentence for your paragraph.

6 Now write your first draft about your special possession. Include a topic sentence that gives the main idea of your paragraph. Write sentences to explain or support the main idea. Don't worry about grammar yet. Just try to make your ideas clear.

REVISE: Staying on the Topic

All the sentences in a paragraph explain and support the main idea. Sentences about other ideas or topics do not belong. Read the paragraph. The topic sentence is underlined. One sentence is not about the main idea. It is crossed out.

> <u>One of my special possessions is a painting by my grandfather.</u> He was not a professional painter, but he painted as a hobby. ~~My sister also paints.~~ The painting is a picture of the house where my father grew up. The house is yellow, and there are trees around it. My grandfather gave me the painting before he died. I think of him when I look at this special painting.

1 Read the paragraph. Underline the topic sentence. Cross out one sentence that is not about the main idea. Then work with a partner. Explain why you chose that sentence to cross out.

> My bicycle is a very special possession. My bike is not worth a lot of money. It is old, but it is in good condition. I ride my bike every day. I ride it to school, to the store, and to my grandmother's house. I walk to these places in the summer. I can go wherever I want because I have a bike.

2 Now go back to the first draft of your paragraph. Does your paragraph have a topic sentence? Do all the sentences explain and support the main idea of the paragraph? Cross out the sentences that are not about the main idea. If necessary, write new sentences. Try to use the grammar and a few of the vocabulary items from this unit in your paragraph.

Go to **MyEnglishLab** for more skill practice.

EDIT: Writing the Final Draft

APPLY Write the final draft of your paragraph. Check your grammar, spelling, capitalization, and punctuation. Be sure to use some of the grammar and vocabulary from the unit. Use the checklist to help you write your final draft.

> **FINAL DRAFT CHECKLIST**
> - ☐ Did you begin with a good topic sentence?
> - ☐ Do the other sentences explain or support the topic sentence?
> - ☐ Did you use the correct form of simple present verbs?
> - ☐ Did you use vocabulary from the unit?

ALTERNATIVE WRITING TOPIC

APPLY Ask someone about his or her favorite possession or collection. Write a paragraph about the person's answer. Use vocabulary and grammar from the unit.

CHECK WHAT YOU'VE LEARNED

Check (✔) the outcomes you've met and vocabulary you've learned. Put an X next to the skills and vocabulary you still need to practice.

Learning Outcomes
- ☐ Infer outcomes
- ☐ List main ideas in notes
- ☐ Identify suggestions
- ☐ Use simple present
- ☐ Write a topic sentence
- ☐ Write supporting sentences
- ☐ Write a descriptive paragraph

Vocabulary
- ☐ collections
- ☐ condition
- ☐ experts AWL
- ☐ favorite
- ☐ guests
- ☐ items AWL
- ☐ rare
- ☐ sentimental
- ☐ valuable, value
- ☐ worth

Go to **MyEnglishLab** to watch a video about a stolen wedding dress, access the Unit Project, and take the Unit 3 Achievement Test.

LEARNING OUTCOMES

- Infer tone
- Take notes on examples
- Use content clues
- Use *There Is / There Are*
- Use adjectives in descriptions
- Write a descriptive paragraph

Go to **MyEnglishLab** to check what you know.

UNIT 4

Open for Business

1 FOCUS ON THE TOPIC

1. What are some different kinds of stores in your neighborhood?
2. Think of one big store and one small store. How are they different? What kinds of things do they sell?

2 FOCUS ON READING

READING ONE | Mom & Pop vs. Big Box

VOCABULARY

1 Read the list of words and their definitions.

customer: a person who buys things in a store; a shopper

price: the money that you pay to buy something

employee: a person who works in a store or business

products: things a person makes and sells

own: to have something that is yours

service: work that someone does for you

owner: someone who owns something

shop: go to a store in order to buy things; a small store

personal attention: special help or service that someone gives you

shopping: the activity of going to stores to buy things

Go to the **Pearson Practice English App** or **MyEnglishLab** for more vocabulary practice.

2 Complete the text with words from the list.

customers • ~~own~~ • personal attention • products • shop
employees • owner • prices • service • shopping

REE'S MENSWEAR
IF YOU LOOK BAD, WE LOOK BAD!

I'm Alexander Ree, and I **own** (1) Ree's Menswear. At Ree's Menswear, we care about you, our **customers** (2).

We give **personal attention** (3) to every customer who visits our store. Our **employees** (4) always give friendly **service** (5) so you feel happy in our **shop** (6).

We have good **prices** (7), so you save money.

Most importantly, we sell excellent **products** (8). When you buy something from Ree's Menswear, you will enjoy it for life.

I always say, "If you look bad, we look bad!"

Thank you for **shopping** (9) at Ree's Menswear.

Alexander Ree

Alexander Ree

Owner (10) of Ree's Menswear

Visit us in one of our stores, or visit us online at **reesmenswear.com**.

PREVIEW

1 You are going to read an article about business. First, look at the photos and read about two different kinds of stores. Then complete the chart.

A **chain store** has many stores with the same name. 7-Eleven® and Starbucks® are chain stores. Large companies usually own chain stores. Some chain stores are called "big box" stores because they are very big and sell many different products. Wal-Mart® and IKEA® are examples of big-box chain stores.

A **locally-owned store** usually has only one or two locations. The owner often lives in the community or not far away. Sometimes, a locally-owned business is called a "mom and pop" store because a family owns it.

2 What are the benefits (good points) and drawbacks (bad points) of shopping at the two kinds of stores? Add your ideas to the chart.

Small, Locally-Owned Stores		Big-Box Chain Stores	
Benefits	Drawbacks	Benefits	Drawbacks
The service is good.	They don't have all the things I want.	They have more products.	The service isn't good.

READ

Read the online article. Create a chart like the one below to take notes. On the left, put the main ideas. On the right, put the details.

TAKE NOTES

Main Ideas	Details
People disagree about stores.	Mom and pop stores or big box stores
Mom and pop stores:	
Big box stores:	
Reader ideas:	

Go to **MyEnglishLab** to view example notes.

E-Business Magazine

The Debate[1] Space: Mom & Pop vs. Big Box

1. Today's debate topic: Is it better to **shop** at mom and pop stores and not at big-box stores?

2. **Please Shop at a Mom and Pop!**
by Patty Sanders

3. Locally-owned stores are important for our community. We are in big trouble if we lose our locally-owned businesses—we need to keep them.

4. At mom and pop stores, **customers** feel like family. **Owners** and **employees** remember the regular customers. They also know every product. They can talk to customers about the **products**. This **personal attention** makes the local community strong. We don't get this personal attention at big-box stores. Large chain stores often have more products and lower **prices** than mom and pop shops. But the personal attention at mom and pop stores is worth a little extra money.

5. How can our community live without locally-owned businesses? Large chain stores do not care about our families—we are not important to them. They care about making money. We can't lose our mom and pop stores. If the locally-owned businesses die, our community will die, too!

6. **Big-Box Stores Aren't the Bad Guy**
by Butch Baker

7. The fact is: People need to save money so they will have it when they need it. Who cares about friendly **service**? People want low prices! Big-box stores have low prices because they sell more products. People want to save money. That's all!

8. **Shopping** at big-box stores is also more convenient. That is, big-box stores make life easier because they have more products. It's one-stop shopping. At my Wal-Mart® Supercenter I can get food, clothes, gas for my car, and much more. Why stop at five different stores if I can stop at just one? That's crazy.

9. Big-box stores are always less expensive and more convenient. People who say big-box stores are bad are totally wrong.

10. **READER COMMENTS:**

11. Not all mom and pop employees are friendly and helpful. And not all big-box stores are cold and impersonal. Both have benefits. —*Caroline*   REPLY

12. National and international chain stores bring jobs to the community, but the pay is very low. Many families don't make enough money to live. —*Albert Chow, CPA*   REPLY

13. I shop where the prices are low and the store hours are convenient. I'm too busy to worry about "mom and pop." —*Mr. Mom*   REPLY

14. At Brooklyn Market we sell fresh food from local farms. We **own** a small store that helps our community. And the people in our community help each other. —*Melissa and Gail*   REPLY

---

[1] **debate:** two or more people giving different opinions about a topic

MAIN IDEAS

1 Look again at your predictions in the Preview section on page 74. Add information from the reading to the chart on page 74.

2 Which writer agrees with these statements? Write the sentences in the correct box.

- Customers care about good prices.
- It is important for employees to speak to customers and help them.
- Locally-owned businesses are important for the community.
- Large chain stores make life easier for customers.

Patty Sanders	Butch Baker
•	•
•	•

DETAILS

1 Complete each sentence with a name from the reading.

| Patty Sanders | Caroline | Mr. Mom |
| Butch Baker | Albert Chow | Melissa and Gail |

1. _____ enjoys personal attention when she shops.
2. _____ is worried about employees' low pay at chain stores.
3. _____ isn't interested in personal attention when he shops.
4. _____ likes both locally-owned stores and big-box stores.
5. _____ own a store that sells food.
6. _____ doesn't have a lot of time to shop.

2 Look at your notes and at your answers in the Preview section. How did they help you understand this article?

MAKE INFERENCES 🔍

Inferring Tone

An **inference** is **an educated guess** about something. The information is **not stated directly** in the reading. Good readers put ideas together to find the answers. **Tone** shows emotion. When you speak, your friends know your emotions because of your words and the sound, or tone, of your voice. When you read, you must infer the tone because you can't hear the writer's voice.

A writer's "voice" can sound happy, angry, or worried. It can also sound *neutral* (no specific emotion).

Look at the example and answer the questions. Then read the explanation.

Reread *"Please Shop at a Mom and Pop!"* by Patty Sanders on page 75. What is the feeling or emotion in her words? Circle the best one.

a. angry
b. sad
c. happy
d. worried
e. confused

What words or phrases in the reading show this emotion? Underline them.

The best answer is *d*. Patty Sanders sounds worried. We know this because she uses words and phrases such as:

- We are in **big trouble** if we lose our locally-owned businesses.
- **How can our community live** without locally-owned businesses?
- We **can't lose** our mom and pop shops.
- If the locally-owned businesses die, our **community will die**, too!

From these boldfaced words and phrases, we can infer that Patty Sanders' tone is worried.

1 Read Butch Baker's opinion in Reading One. What is his tone? Circle the best answer. Underline words or phrases in the reading that express his tone.

a. angry

b. sad

c. happy

d. worried

e. confused

f. neutral

2 Look at Reading One again. Answer the questions.

1 Which writer uses a neutral tone? _____

2 How do you know? _____

Open for Business   **77**

DISCUSS

1 Work with a partner. What do Patty Sanders and Butch Baker think? Complete the sentences. Find the information in Reading One to support your answers.

USE YOUR NOTES

Use your notes to support your answers with information from the reading.

Patty Sanders:

- I prefer to shop at _____

    because _____ is most

    important to me. I go to a store if _____ .

Butch Baker:

- I prefer to shop at _____ because

    _____ is most important to me. I go to

    a store if _____ .

2 Do you agree more with Butch or Patty? Why?

Go to **MyEnglishLab** to give your opinion about another question.

READING TWO | Etsy.com

PREVIEW

1 Look at the title of the reading and the pictures. Write two questions that you think will be answered in this reading.

_____

_____

2 Look at the boldfaced words in the reading. Which words do you already know? What does each word mean?

READ

1 Read the magazine article about an online company. As you read, guess the meaning of the words that are new to you. Remember to take notes on main ideas and details.

Profiles: Etsy.com

Do you see the same products in every store? Do you want **unique** items—things that are different and one-of-a-kind? My answer is "Yes!" And that is why I shop at Etsy.com®.

Etsy is an online **marketplace**—people can buy many unique things there. But Etsy is different. It is not just another Amazon.com® or eBay®.

First, I can find unique items from all over the world. Customers buy **crafts**, such as handmade jewelry and furniture. They also find other rare products, such as watches and old, vintage clothing.[1] You can't find these items in stores, certainly not in big-box stores. I love that!

Second, when I shop at Etsy, I know I am helping the **vendors**, the individuals who sell things. Most of these vendors are the **artisans**, that is, the people who make their items by hand. They care about their crafts, their business, and their customers.

Lastly, the customer service is great. I get all the benefits of shopping at locally-owned businesses. I can ask the vendors questions online, and they quickly answer me. Also, my items arrive carefully wrapped[2] by the craftsperson, not by a machine.

There is one small disadvantage. Because the items are unique or handmade, sometimes it is not possible to return them to the vendor. That is an advantage of a big-box store. (But I am happy with everything from Etsy.)

Online shopping is usually fast but not very personal. Etsy changes that. It is convenient and fast, but it is also personal. Etsy brings people together. This makes Etsy unique and exciting.

Visit Etsy.com and see for yourself.

[1] **vintage clothing:** clothing from a past time that other people owned before
[2] **wrapped:** covered with pretty paper

| Furniture | Vintage clothing | Jewelry | Custom gift wrap |

2 Compare your notes on main ideas and details with a partner's. How can you improve your notes next time?

Go to the **Pearson Practice English App** or **MyEnglishLab** for more vocabulary practice.

Open for Business

NOTE-TAKING SKILL

Noting Examples

An example is one item in a group.

Idea or Group	Examples
Chain stores	IKEA, 7-Eleven, Starbucks, Wal-Mart
Universities	Yonsei University, Columbia University, Oxford University, Nanyang Technological University

Separate examples with comma (,).

When you take notes, you can abbreviate "for example" with "e.g.," (which is short for *exempli gratia* in Latin). Also, put your examples in parentheses (e.g., . . .).

Long form: People shop at chain stores, for example, IKEA, 7-Eleven, Starbucks, and Wal-Mart.

Short form: Chain stores (e.g., IKEA, 7-Eleven, Starbucks, Wal-Mart)

1 Give examples of each of the following ideas or groups. Use the short form.

1. There are several stores near my school (e.g., _____).

2. When I go to the supermarket, I buy many different kinds of foods _____.

3. I use apps on my phone _____.

2 Look at Reading 2 again. In your notebook, make a chart that looks like the one below. Then complete the chart.

TAKE NOTES

Main Ideas	Examples
Reasons to shop on Etsy?	e.g., unique items, helps vendors and crafts people . . .
Things you can buy on Etsy:	
Benefits for the customer of shopping on Etsy:	

Go to **MyEnglishLab** to view example notes.

COMPREHENSION

1 Complete the sentences with information from the reading.

1. Etsy is _____

2. The vendors are _____

3. Customers can _____

4. Shopping on Etsy is _____

2 Review the boldfaced words from the reading with a partner. Use a dictionary or ask your teacher for any meanings you still do not know.

READING SKILL

1 Look at Reading Two again. Find the words in the text. Then choose the correct definition of each word. Write the letter on the line. Do not use a dictionary.

Then, in the text, underline the words, phrases, and punctuation that helped you understand the words.

Words	Definitions
____ 1. unique (paragraph 1)	a. a space where people buy and sell things
____ 2. marketplace (paragraph 2)	b. people who make things by hand
____ 3. crafts (paragraph 3)	c. people who sell things
____ 4. vendors (paragraph 4)	d. things made by hand using special talent or skill
____ 5. artisans (paragraph 4)	e. special or different from other things

Using Context Clues

Sometimes you can find the meaning of a word from the **context,** or the words, phrases, and sentences around the word. These helpful words, phrases, or sentences are called **context clues.**

Commas or dashes can suggest a context clue. Above, the phrase *or the words, phrases, and sentences around the word* explains the word *context*. It helps you understand what *context* means.

That is, . . . can suggest an explanation or context clue.

Such as . . . (followed by examples) can also suggest a context clue.

For example, the word *unique* in paragraph 1 means "one-of-a-kind." The context clue is "—things that are different or one-of-a-kind." The dash (—) suggests the context clue.

(continued on next page)

Look at these other examples:

marketplace
context clue: "—people can buy many unique things there."

crafts
context clue: "such as handmade jewelry and furniture."

vendors
context clue: "vendors, the individuals who sell things."

artisans
context clue: "that is, the people who make their items by hand."

2 Look at Reading One on page 75 again. Find the words in the text. Then choose the correct definition of each word. Write the letter on the line. Do not use a dictionary.

Then, in the text, underline the words, phrases, and punctuation that helped you understand the words.

Words

_____ 1. lose (paragraph 3)

_____ 2. care (paragraph 5)

_____ 3. save (paragraph 7)

_____ 4. convenient (paragraph 8)

Definitions

a. useful or easy

b. not have something any more

c. think that something is important

d. keep something so you can use it later

Go to **MyEnglishLab** for more skill practice.

CONNECT THE READINGS

ORGANIZE

USE YOUR NOTES

Use your notes from Reading One and the information from Reading Two to complete the chart.

Check (✓) the benefits of each kind of business.

	Mom and Pop Stores	Big-Box Chain Stores	Etsy.com
LOW PRICES			
MANY DIFFERENT PRODUCTS			
UNIQUE ITEMS			
HANDMADE GOODS			
PERSONAL ATTENTION			
KNOWLEDGEABLE STAFF			
CONVENIENCE			
EASY COMMUNICATION			
OTHER _____			

SYNTHESIZE

1 Imagine you are starting a business. What ideas from the readings are important to you? Complete a short business plan describing your business or service.

1. What is the product or service?
   _____

2. How much is it?
   _____

3. Who are your customers?
   _____

4. Where will you sell this product or service?
   _____

   _____ online

   _____ in a small store

   _____ in a chain store

2 In your notebook, write a short paragraph about your business. Use the information from the chart.

Go to **MyEnglishLab** to check what you learned.

3 FOCUS ON WRITING

VOCABULARY

REVIEW

Complete the passage. Write the correct word on the line.

Hi. My name is Judy. I am an _____ , and I sell my handmade jewelry—mostly
1. (artisan / employee)

earrings and necklaces—on Etsy. For many years I made jewelry in my free time. Then my friends

said, "Those are beautiful! You should sell them." Now I do. I am the _____ of a
2. (product / owner)

small business on Etsy. I opened my Etsy _____ in September last year.
3. (shop / customer)

I enjoy being a _____ on Etsy. I have a full-time job during the day. I'm a
4. (vendor / customer)

waitress. At night and on weekends, I make jewelry and run my business. Etsy makes this

possible for me. I have no _____ . I make everything by myself. I am very busy,
5. (employees / crafts)

but I love it.

Today my business is growing. I sell my products in an international _____ ,
6. (service / marketplace)

not just local. I have _____ in my neighborhood and around the world. I can
7. (prices / customers)

communicate with people around the world.

I care about my jewelry. I enjoy making and

selling it to people. With Etsy, I can give my

customers _____—even if
8. (personal attention / marketplaces)

I can't meet them face-to-face.

Are the holidays coming? Or your mother's

birthday? Try _____
9. (shopping / selling)

online at Etsy. You'll find thousands of

_____ items for someone
10. (free / unique)

special. Be sure to visit Judy's Jewels while

you are on Etsy.

84   UNIT 4

EXPAND

GERUNDS

A *gerund* is a noun that ends in *-ing*.

Gerunds name activities, such as *shopping, speaking,* or *riding.* In a sentence, a gerund can be a subject or an object.

For example:

[subject]
Movies are fun.

[gerund subject]
Going to the movies is fun.

[object]
Sofia enjoys movies.

[gerund object]
Sofia enjoys going to movies.

Verbs such as *enjoy* and *spend time* often have a gerund as an object.

Note: A *gerund phrase* is a gerund + the words that go with it.

Sofia enjoys *going to movies.*   Riding a bicycle is good exercise.

1 Match the beginning of the sentence with the end. Write the letter on the line.

Subject

		Verb + Object
_e_	1. Owning a business . . .	a. is interesting sometimes.
____	2. Shopping online . . .	b. but it is not the most important thing in life.
____	3. Saving money in the bank . . .	c. is important for your future.
____	4. Making money is important, . . .	d. is very convenient.
____	5. Communicating with people from other countries . . .	e. is hard work for the owner.

Subject + Verb

		Object
____	6. Every morning, I enjoy . . .	f. going to the dentist.
____	7. My hobby is . . .	g. collecting coins.
____	8. I don't like . . .	h. reading the newspaper online.
____	9. My little sister likes . . .	i. riding our bikes around the city.
____	10. We spend a lot of time . . .	j. playing with her toys.

2 Complete each sentence with a gerund or gerund phrase.

1. I enjoy _____ .
2. _____ is one of my favorite things to do.
3. I don't enjoy _____ .
4. _____ is really boring.
5. I spend a lot of time _____ .

CREATE

APPLY Work with two or three partners. Write phrases and sentences to complete the journalist's interviews. Use vocabulary words from the box. Then present your conversation to the class.

artisans	marketplace	personal attention	shop
crafts	own	prices	shopping
customers	owner	product	unique
employees	owning	service	vendors

WAYLON FLUFFINGS: Good morning. This is Waylon Fluffings for *The Morning Report*. I'm reporting from the outdoor market in Prospect Park in Brooklyn, New York. Let's talk to one of the vendors here, Madeline Ortiz, from Salem Farms. Hello, Ms. Ortiz. You work for Salem Farms . . .

MADELINE ORTIZ: Well, actually I'm not just an employee. I'm the _____

WF: Oh, sorry. My mistake. What do you sell? And why do you think customers shop here?

MO: _____
_____

WF: Thanks very much for speaking with us, Ms. Ortiz. And now, let's talk to some shoppers. Here are Jeanne Lambert and Laszlo Arvai. Ms. Lambert, why do you come to this market?

JEANNE LAMBERT: Well, _____
_____

WF: And, Mr. Arvai, do you enjoy shopping here?

LASZLO ARVAI: Usually I don't like shopping, but I do enjoy _____ here. I just bought (a / some) _____ as a gift for my mother. It's _____

WF: That's great. Thank you both very much. I'm Waylon Fluffings, and it's a beautiful morning here in Brooklyn's Prospect Park, so come on down and check out this amazing marketplace.

Go to the **Pearson Practice English App** or **MyEnglishLab** for more vocabulary practice.

GRAMMAR FOR WRITING

1 Read the email from Young-Hee to her friend from university, Sofia. Answer the questions. Then discuss your answers with a partner.

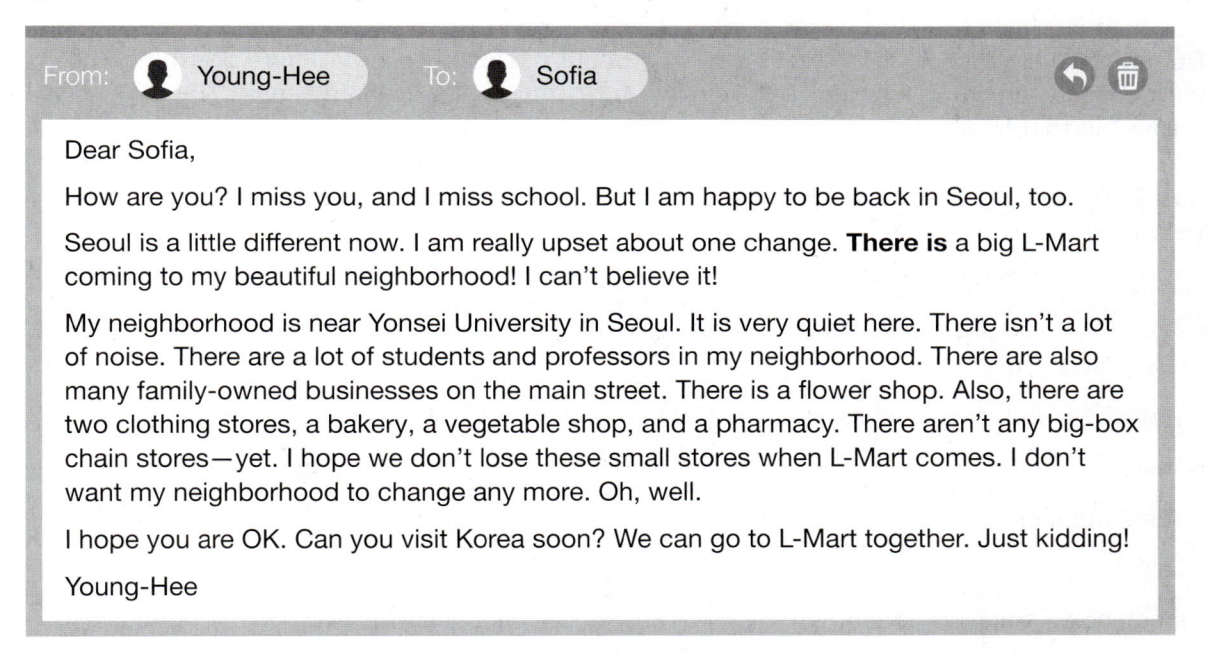

From: Young-Hee   To: Sofia

Dear Sofia,

How are you? I miss you, and I miss school. But I am happy to be back in Seoul, too.

Seoul is a little different now. I am really upset about one change. **There is** a big L-Mart coming to my beautiful neighborhood! I can't believe it!

My neighborhood is near Yonsei University in Seoul. It is very quiet here. There isn't a lot of noise. There are a lot of students and professors in my neighborhood. There are also many family-owned businesses on the main street. There is a flower shop. Also, there are two clothing stores, a bakery, a vegetable shop, and a pharmacy. There aren't any big-box chain stores—yet. I hope we don't lose these small stores when L-Mart comes. I don't want my neighborhood to change any more. Oh, well.

I hope you are OK. Can you visit Korea soon? We can go to L-Mart together. Just kidding!

Young-Hee

1. How many times does Young-Hee use *there is*, *there isn't*, *there are*, and *there aren't*? Underline them.
2. What nouns follow *there is* and *there isn't*? Make a list.
3. What nouns follow *there are* and *there aren't*? Make a list.

There Is / There Are

1. Use **there is** or **there are** to state facts about something in the **present**. Note: A count noun is a person place or thing that we can count (one street, two streets). A non-count noun cannot be counted (traffic). *There is* + singular count noun *There are* + plural count noun *There is* + non-count noun	 **There is a bank** on Main Street. **There are a lot of students** in my neighborhood. **There is a lot of traffic** in Seoul.
2. Use **there was** or **there were** to state facts about something in the past.	**There was** a flower shop on my street. **There were** a lot of people on my street.
3. Use the contractions **isn't / aren't** and **wasn't / weren't** with **there** in the **negative**.	**There isn't** a McDonald's® nearby. **There weren't** any big-box chain stores.
4. For **questions**, put **there** after **is / are** and **was / were**. Use **any** with **yes / no** questions about **plural nouns** and **non-count nouns**.	**Is there** a movie theater nearby? **Were there any restaurants** in your neighborhood? **Is there any traffic** in your neighborhood at night?
5. Do not confuse *there is* and *there are* with *there* when you refer to place. *There* means "in that location."	Seoul is a beautiful city. **There are** some beautiful parks **there** (in Seoul).

2 Read Sofia's reply to Young-Hee. Then choose the correct verbs to complete her sentences.

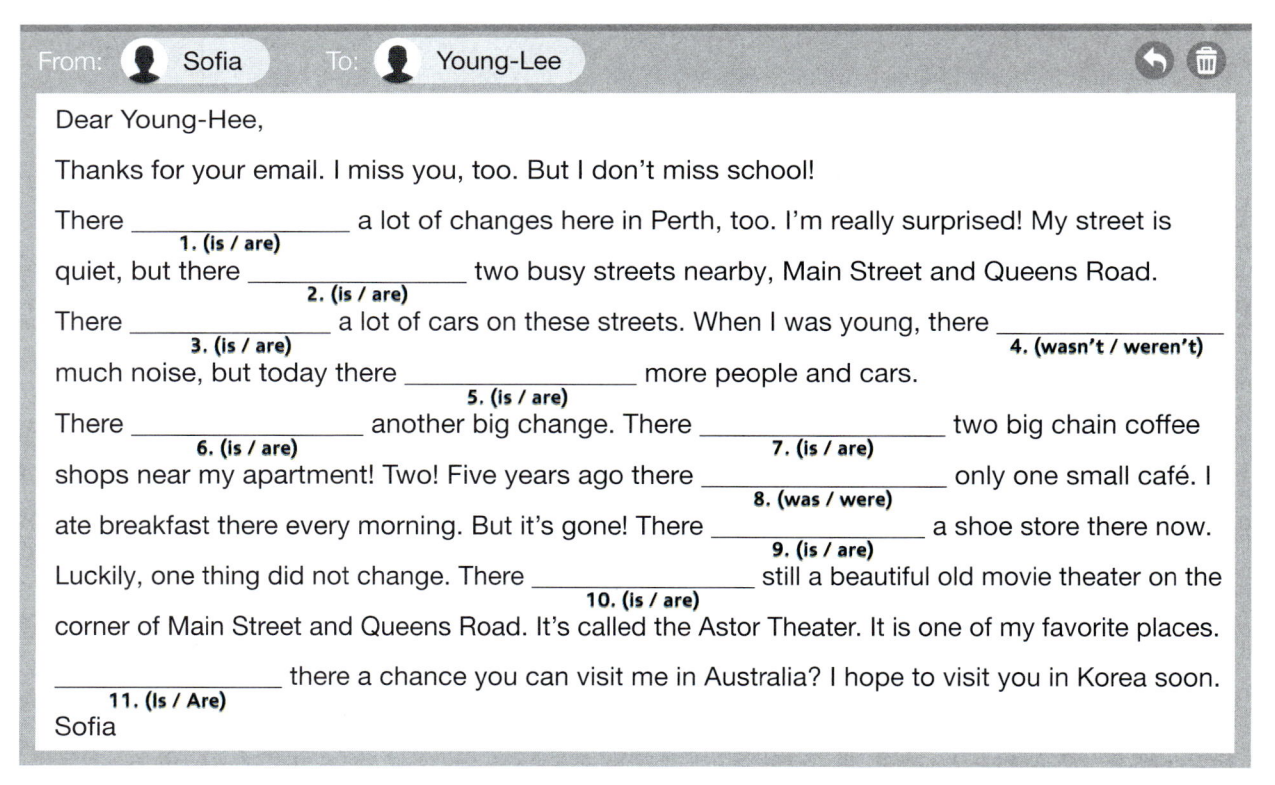

From: Sofia   To: Young-Lee

Dear Young-Hee,

Thanks for your email. I miss you, too. But I don't miss school!

There _____ a lot of changes here in Perth, too. I'm really surprised! My street is
        1. (is / are)
quiet, but there _____ two busy streets nearby, Main Street and Queens Road.
              2. (is / are)
There _____ a lot of cars on these streets. When I was young, there _____
    3. (is / are)   **4. (wasn't / weren't)**
much noise, but today there _____ more people and cars.
                          5. (is / are)
There _____ another big change. There _____ two big chain coffee
    6. (is / are)   **7. (is / are)**
shops near my apartment! Two! Five years ago there _____ only one small café. I
                                                    8. (was / were)
ate breakfast there every morning. But it's gone! There _____ a shoe store there now.
                                                          9. (is / are)
Luckily, one thing did not change. There _____ still a beautiful old movie theater on the
                                         10. (is / are)
corner of Main Street and Queens Road. It's called the Astor Theater. It is one of my favorite places.

_____ there a chance you can visit me in Australia? I hope to visit you in Korea soon.
11. (Is / Are)
Sofia

3 APPLY Work with a partner. Write five questions to ask about your partner's neighborhood or city. Use *Is / Are there* and *Was / Were there.* Then exchange books and answer each other's questions. Use *There is / are* and *There was / were*.

1. a. *Is there a fast food restaurant nearby?*
   b. *Yes, there is. There is a McDonald's and a Subway.*
2. a. _____
   b. _____
3. a. _____
   b. _____
4. a. _____
   b. _____
5. a. _____
   b. _____
6. a. _____
   b. _____

> Go to the **Pearson Practice English App** or **MyEnglishLab** for more grammar practice. Check what you learned in **MyEnglishLab**.

FINAL WRITING TASK: A Descriptive Paragraph   APPLY

In this unit, you read about locally-owned stores and large chain stores. You also read about the online marketplace, Etsy.

You are going to **write a paragraph describing a business that you recommend or a place where you like to shop.** Use the vocabulary and grammar from the unit.

For an alternative writing topic, see page 93.

PREPARE TO WRITE: Brainstorming

1 Think about the different stores or businesses where you usually shop. Think only about brick-and-mortar stores (physical places), not online stores. Make a list in the chart under Business.

Business	Local?	Chain?	Big Box?	Notes

Open for Business

2 Now complete the chart. Check the appropriate boxes: Local, Chain, or Big-Box. Under Notes, write notes about this store. Then tell a partner about the stores.

3 Choose one place that you think is most interesting. You will write about this one.

4 In your notebook, answer some of these questions:

1. Is it a big-box store or a locally-owned business?
2. How convenient is it to shop there?
3. Who are the customers?
4. Who are the owners? Who are the employees?
5. What product or service does this business sell?
6. If I go there, what will I see?
7. When is this business open? What are the hours?
8. Where is this business?
9. Why do I like it?
10. How is the service? How are the prices?

Note: You don't have to use all the information from your questions. Use the information that you think is most important when you write your paragraph.

WRITE: Describing a place

When you describe something, organize the information for the reader. One way you can organize is to use an idea or a feeling. For example, if your favorite store is a "happy" place, describe all the things there that make you feel happy.

Example

> I always enjoy shopping for food at Sunshine Market. The space feels happy. The walls are painted yellow and green—bright, happy colors. There is a lot of light from the big windows. If you can't find something, you can ask the employees. There aren't any unfriendly employees there. They are all very helpful and friendly. They smile a lot. I think they enjoy working there. The prices are also lower than other food stores. That really makes me happy. Visit Sunshine Market when you are in my neighborhood.

You can also organize by telling where things are—space organization. For example, you can write about what you see when you walk into the room. You can describe what you see when you look from right to left or left to right.

Example

> I always enjoy shopping at Veronica's. The store has a lot of unique items in the window. When you walk in, you see a big table on the left. It has unusual jewelry and other handmade things. On the right, there is a section called "Artisans' Marketplace." There is beautiful handmade clothing for men and women from all over the world. Shopping at Veronica's is interesting and fun. I highly recommend it.

Notice that the second paragraph has a clear description of what the writer sees. The description also shows the writer's feeling that the shop is "interesting and fun."

1 Read the paragraph. Then answer the questions in your notebook.

> "That's Amore" is my favorite restaurant. My husband and I like to go there. It's small and romantic. There are only ten tables along the wall. They are not too close together, so customers can talk easily. The lights are not too bright, but they are not too dark. There is a candle on every table. They give the room a warm feeling. The kitchen is always very busy, but it is clean. "Amore" is Italian for "love." It's easy to feel the love at "That's Amore." Go there with someone you love.

1. What "feeling(s)" does the writer want to communicate? How do you know?
2. Which sentence does not belong in this description? Why?

2 Imagine you are a sitting in a fast food chain restaurant, such as McDonald's® or KFC®. Answer the questions in your notebook. Then write a short descriptive paragraph about the restaurant. Be sure to organize your ideas and to focus on a feeling.

1. What are some things that you see? Make a list of five things.
2. What is the feeling you get from being there?

3 Now write the first draft of your paragraph about a business or place where you like to shop. Don't worry about the grammar. Just try to make the ideas clear.

REVISE

Using Adjectives in Descriptions

A simple **adjective** is a word that modifies, or describes, a noun.

    a **helpful** employee   **low** prices   a **beautiful** shop

When you describe something in writing, use adjectives that show how things look, feel, smell, taste, or sound.

Prepositional phrases can help to add details and show location. A prepositional phrase is a group of words that begin with a preposition (*in, on, at, between, from,* etc.).

    candles **on** every table

    tables **along** the wall

    a handsome man **in** a really nice suit

    across the top **of** the page

    from left **to** right

Open for Business

1 Read the paragraph. Underline seven more simple adjectives.

> BuyBooks.com is a <u>terrible</u> website. I do not recommend it. First, it is very slow. Most websites are very fast—just click, click, click, and you are finished. BuyBooks.com is different. I was on BuyBooks.com for 15 minutes to buy just a book. Second, it is a very confusing website. Next time, I will go to a better website or to a brick-and-mortar bookstore.

2 Complete the paragraph with the words or phrases from the box.

| comfortable | friendly | huge | ~~interesting~~ | near my house | next to the window |

> I recommend The Night Owl Bookshop. It is a great place to buy books. It is open late at night. It has a lot of ____interesting____ books. For example, it has a _____
> 1.   2.
> collection of comic books. I also like the feeling in The Night Owl Bookshop. There are a lot of
> _____ chairs. My favorite chair is _____. The employees
>   3.   4.
> are very _____. They always say hello. I'm glad that The Night Owl Bookshop is
>   5.
> _____. I think you should go there.
>   6.

3 Look at the first draft of your paragraph. Underline the descriptive adjectives and prepositional phrases you used. Add descriptive adjectives and prepositional phrases where you can.

🔗 Go to **MyEnglishLab** for more skill practice.

EDIT: Writing the Final Draft

APPLY Write the final draft of your paragraph. Check your grammar, spelling, capitalization, and punctuation. Be sure to use some of the grammar and vocabulary from the unit. Use the checklist to help you write your final draft.

> **FINAL DRAFT CHECKLIST**
>
> ☐ Did you describe a business?
> ☐ Did you begin with a good topic sentence?
> ☐ Did you use *there is / are* correctly?
> ☐ Did you use descriptive adjectives and prepositional phrases?
> ☐ Did you use vocabulary from the unit?

ALTERNATIVE WRITING TOPIC

APPLY In many places, large businesses are becoming more popular. Small, locally-owned businesses are going out of business. Is this a good change? Why or why not? Write your answer in one paragraph. Use vocabulary and grammar from the unit.

CHECK WHAT YOU'VE LEARNED

Check (✔) the outcomes you've met and vocabulary you've learned. Put an X next to the skills and vocabulary you still need to practice.

Learning Outcomes
☐ Infer tone
☐ Take notes on examples
☐ Use context clues
☐ Use *There is / There are*
☐ Use adjectives in descriptions
☐ Write a descriptive paragraph

Vocabulary
☐ artisan
☐ collecting
☐ crafts
☐ customer
☐ employee
☐ making
☐ marketplace
☐ own, owner, owning
☐ price
☐ product
☐ reading
☐ saving
☐ service
☐ shop, shopping
☐ unique AWL
☐ vendor

Multi-word Units
☐ personal attention

➤ Go to **MyEnglishLab** to watch a video about selling hot dogs, access the Unit Project, and take the Unit 4 Achievement Test.

LEARNING OUTCOMES

- Infer meaning
- Note definitions
- Identify causes and effects
- Use basic modals (*can, may, will, might*)
- Add supporting details
- Write suggestions

Go to **MyEnglishLab** to check what you know.

UNIT 5
What Are You Afraid Of?

1 FOCUS ON THE TOPIC

1. What do you see in the photo?
2. How do people feel about the thing in the photo?
3. What are some other things that people fear, perhaps for no reason?

2 FOCUS ON READING

READING ONE | Help! I'm Scared!

VOCABULARY

1 Read the list of words, definitions, and sentences.

afraid (of): scared of something that may hurt you. *I am afraid of spiders.*

fear (N): a feeling of great worry. *I have a fear of snakes.*

fear (V): be afraid of someone or something. *I fear snakes.*

panic: suddenly feel afraid and do things quickly without thinking. *People panic when someone cries "Fire!"*

avoid: stay away from someone or something. *I avoid scary neighborhoods at night.*

embarrassed: feeling worried and unhappy about what other people think of you. *I feel embarrassed when everyone looks at me.*

relaxed: calm and not worried. *They feel very relaxed on the beach.*

normal: usual or expected. *It's normal to feel afraid sometimes. Everyone does.*

phobia: a very strong fear of something that stops you from doing things. *I have a phobia of snakes.*

2 Use the words from the list to complete the poster.

DO YOU HAVE A PHOBIA?

- Are you ____*afraid*____ of something?
  1.
- Do you have a _____ of spiders, snakes, airplanes?
  2.
- Do you ever _____ when you're in a large crowd of people?
  3.
- Do you _____ places or things because you're scared?
  4.
- Do you feel _____ because other people laugh at your fear?
  5.
- Do you ever think, I just want to feel _____ again, like other people?
  6.

If you said "yes" to these questions, then you may have a _____.
  7.

Don't let a phobia stop you! You can feel happy and _____ again.
  8.

Visit www.askdoctorperry.com.com for more information.

Go to the **Pearson Practice English App** or **MyEnglishLab** for more vocabulary practice.

PREVIEW

You are going to read part of a website called *askdoctorperry.com*. On this website, Dr. Hope Perry helps people when they are worried or sick. Dr. Perry got an email from Ann because Ann has a fear of spiders.

What will Dr. Perry say to Ann? Check (✓) the answers you think are correct.

_____ "Most spiders cannot hurt you."

_____ "Your fear is not normal."

_____ "Try to relax."

_____ "Read about spiders."

_____ Your ideas: _____

READ

Read the website. In your notebook, create a chart like the one below to take notes. On the left, put the main ideas. On the right, put the details.

TAKE NOTES	
Main Ideas	**Details**
Ann has arachnophobia	afraid of spiders, feels afraid all the time, can't sleep, avoids attic, feels embarrassed and alone
Phobias	

Go to **MyEnglishLab** to view example notes.

What Are You Afraid Of?

Subject: Help! I'm Scared!

Dear Dr. Perry,

I have a problem, and I hope you can help me. Last month when I went up into the attic of my house, a big spider fell into my hair. I started to **panic**! I ran from the attic, down into the house, and out the door. My heart was racing,[1] and I felt sick.

Now, I am **afraid** all the time. In the morning I look for spiders in my shoes. At night I can't sleep because a spider may fall in my hair. I **avoid** going to the attic because of spiders. Also, I feel alone. I feel **embarrassed** because my family laughs at me. My family says, "Relax! Spiders are small!" But I never feel **relaxed**. I'm always worried.

Can you help? I need some advice.

Ann

attic

Dear Ann,

I understand. Don't worry. A lot of people **fear** spiders, so being **afraid of** spiders is **normal**. Spiders have many long legs, and people don't like that. Also, their webs look dirty. But most spiders are not dangerous, so they cannot hurt you.

But for some people, a normal fear becomes a **phobia**. When you have a phobia, you cannot have a normal life. You can't do normal things. Other people may laugh at you, but they don't understand your **fear**. Don't be embarrassed.

web

Why do we have phobias? Sometimes they start with a bad experience. Sometimes we learn a fear from our parents. Sometimes there is no reason.

You might have arachnophobia, the fear of spiders. When you see a spider, you might have a panic attack. A panic attack is when your heart beats very fast, or you may feel sick because of fear. It might also be difficult for you to think. You can get help for arachnophobia. Here is some advice:

— Read about spiders, so you will be less afraid of them.
— Look at photos of spiders, both live and dead ones. After some time, you will feel better.
— Try to relax when you see a spider. Think about something nice.
— Talk about your fear with family, friends, or a doctor.

Good luck to you, Ann!

Dr. Perry

---

[1] **racing:** moving very fast

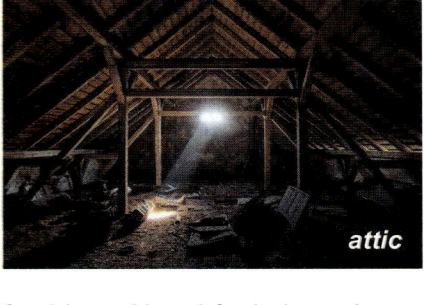

MAIN IDEAS

1. Look again at your predictions in the Preview section on page 97. Circle your predictions that match the information in the reading.

2. Read each sentence. Circle the best answer.

   1. Ann needs help because _____ .
      a. her bedroom has spiders
      b. her fear is a big problem

   2. It is <u>not</u> normal to _____ .
      a. be afraid of spiders
      b. have a phobia of spiders

   3. A phobia means you _____ .
      a. can't do normal things because you are scared
      b. can't do normal things because you are embarrassed

   4. Dr. Perry gives _____ to people with phobias.
      a. medicine
      b. help

DETAILS

1. Read Ann's story again. Find the incorrect word in each sentence. Draw a line through the incorrect word and write the correct word above it.

   (1.) Ann's phobia started when a spider fell in her ~~shoe~~ *hair*. (2.) Now Ann can't eat, and she always feels afraid. (3.) Dr. Perry thinks Ann may have a spider. (4.) Phobias can come from a good experience, parents, or nothing. (5.) When Dr. Perry sees a spider, she may have a panic attack. (6.) That means her heart beats very fast, she feels relaxed, and she can't think. (7.) Dr. Perry tells Ann to read about spiders, look at pictures of spiders, relax, and laugh about the fear.

2. Look at your notes and at your questions from the Preview section. How did they help you understand this website?

MAKE INFERENCES

Inferring Meaning

An **inference** is **an educated guess** about something. The information is **not stated directly** in the reading. Sometimes writers give their ideas directly. For example, in paragraph 2, Ann writes, "Now, I am afraid all the time." When we read Ann's words, we understand that she feels scared. Ann's meaning is clear.

Sometimes writers give their ideas indirectly. Good readers use what they read and what they already know to **infer what the writer means.**

Read the question below and circle the best answer. Then read the explanation.

In paragraph 2, Ann writes, "my family laughs at me. My family says, 'Relax! Spiders are small!'"

What does Ann probably mean?

a. Her family thinks spiders are scary.

b. Her family doesn't think Ann is really afraid.

c. Her family is not afraid of spiders.

We already know that most people do not laugh when they are afraid. We also know that people are usually not relaxed when they are afraid. From what Ann writes, we can *infer* that she means her family is <u>not</u> afraid of spiders. The best answer is **c.**

Read each statement. Circle the correct answer.

1. In paragraph 4, Dr. Perry writes, "Don't worry." What does Dr. Perry probably mean?

    a. "Your fear is silly."

    b. "Being afraid is OK."

    c. "Spiders cannot hurt you."

2. In paragraph 5, Dr. Perry writes, "Don't be embarrassed." What does Dr. Perry probably mean?

    a. "Laughing is fun."

    b. "People will not laugh."

    c. "Your fear is not funny."

3. In paragraph 8, Dr. Perry writes, "Read about spiders, so you will be less afraid." What does Dr. Perry probably mean?

    a. "Books help you feel better."

    b. "You will understand spiders."

    c. "You can learn how to kill spiders."

DISCUSS 🔍

Arachnophobia is only one kind of phobia. Some people are afraid of other things. Look at the list below.

- snakes
- clowns
- going to the dentist
- small spaces
- very high places
- dogs or other animals

a clown

Work with a partner. For each item in the list, discuss phobias by completing one of the sentences. Find information in Reading One to support your answers.

- People may be **afraid of** _____ because . . .
  _____

- I know someone who is **afraid of** _____ because . . .
  _____

- Dr. Perry might say . . .
  _____

Go to **MyEnglishLab** to give your opinion about another question.

READING TWO | Other Phobias

PREVIEW

1. Look at the title of the reading and the pictures. Write four fears that you think will be explained in this reading.

2. Look at the boldfaced words in the reading. Which words do you already know? What does each one mean?

> **USE YOUR NOTES**
>
> Use your notes to support your answers with information from the reading.

What Are You Afraid Of?   101

READ

1 Read about people with other phobias. Remember to take notes on main ideas and details.

OTHER PHOBIAS

Elisa has *ophidiophobia*. *Ophidiophobia* is the fear of snakes. People think snakes are **disgusting** because snakes look dirty and wet. Snakes are not disgusting. They are clean and dry. Most people with a snake phobia have never seen or touched a real snake! These people are afraid, so they avoid parks and other places where snakes live.

Rosa has *acrophobia*. *Acrophobia* is the fear of high places. All people have some fear of high places. When people have acrophobia, they panic. As a result, they can't be in a tall building. They can't walk on a high bridge.

Sam has *trypanophobia*. *Trypanophobia* is the fear of **needles**. This fear usually starts in childhood. When children visit the doctor, they cry because needles hurt. When children are older, they learn to relax. People with a phobia never relax. Because they cannot relax, they panic, or they avoid the doctor.

Ali has *glossophobia*. *Glossophobia* is the fear of public speaking. People with *glossophobia* speak easily with friends and people at work. They panic when a lot of people are watching and listening. They have wet hands because they sweat a lot.

a snake

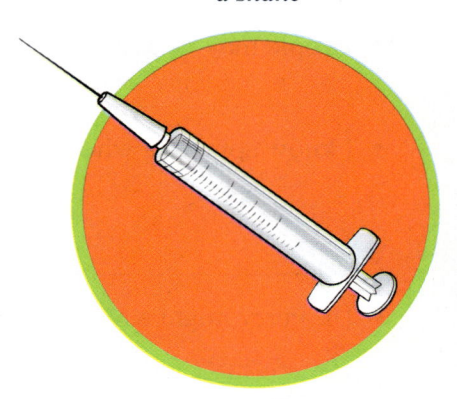

a needle

a man afraid of public speaking

2 Compare your notes on main ideas and details with a partner's. How can you improve your notes next time?

Go to the **Pearson Practice English App** or **MyEnglishLab** for more vocabulary practice.

NOTE-TAKING SKILL

Noting Definitions

You often see new words in a reading. Sometimes the definition of important words is in the reading. When you take notes, keep a list of important words and their definitions. Noting definitions helps you remember and review.

When you note a definition, use a colon (:) or a dash (-). Don't write complete sentences. Write key words from the definition, or explain the definition in your own words.

In Reading One you read "You might have arachnophobia, the fear of spiders." When you take notes, just write:

arachnophobia: fear of spiders

You also read in Reading One, "A panic attack is when your heart beats very fast, or you may feel sick because of fear. It might also be difficult for you to think." In your notes write:

panic attack—heart beats fast, feel sick, can't think

1 Read the paragraph. Then note the important words and their definitions on the lines.

> My sister has a fear of dogs, or *cynophobia*. She is afraid of all dogs: big, small, young, and old. My sister's fear started when she was little. She avoids the park because of her fear. Also, my sister has *germophobia*. *Germophobia* is a fear of germs or sickness. My sister washes her hands a lot. She panics when she is around sick people.

_____

_____

2 Look at Reading Two again. Find the important words. Note the important words and their definitions in your notebook.

Go to **MyEnglishLab** for more note-taking practice.

What Are You Afraid Of?

COMPREHENSION

1 Read the sentences. Write T (true) or F (false). When a sentence is false, cross out the incorrect information and write correct information.

_____ 1. The fear of public speaking usually starts when a child goes to the doctor.

_____ 2. When people have a fear of high places, they panic in tall buildings or on high bridges.

_____ 3. People with a fear of snakes avoid going to the attic.

_____ 4. People with a fear of public speaking panic when they talk to friends or people at work.

2 Review the boldfaced words from the reading with a partner. Use a dictionary or ask your teacher for any meanings you still do not know.

READING SKILL

1 Look at paragraph 1 of Reading Two again. The writer says some people think snakes are disgusting. Based on what you read, why do people think snakes are disgusting? Check (✓) the best answer. Then underline the words or phrases in the text that helped you answer the question.

_____ snakes live in parks and other places

_____ people have *ophidiophobia*

_____ snakes look dirty and wet

Identifying Cause and Effect

When we understand how different ideas connect, we can understand a reading better.

Often, ideas are connected by cause and effect. The cause answers the question, *Why did something happen?* The effect answers the question, *What is the result?*

The word *because* tells you that the writer is stating the cause. *Because* can be at the beginning or end of the sentence. When because comes first, a comma comes after the cause.

[effect] [cause]
People think snakes are disgusting <u>because snakes look dirty and wet</u>.

[cause] [effect]
<u>Because snakes look dirty and wet</u>, people think snakes are disgusting.

The word *so* and the expression *as a result* show that the writer is talking about the effects.

[cause] [effect]
Snakes look dirty and wet, <u>so people think snakes are disgusting</u>.

[cause] [effect]
Snakes look dirty and wet. <u>As a result, people think snakes are disgusting</u>.

2 Use ideas from Reading Two to complete the chart. Underline the words in Reading Two that helped you understand.

Paragraph	Cause	Effect
1	People with a snake phobia are afraid of snakes.	They avoid parks and other places where snakes live.
2	When people have acrophobia, they panic.	They can't be in a tall building. They can't walk on a high bridge.
3		Children cry.
4	People with trypanophobia never relax in a doctor's office.	
5		They have wet hands.

Go to MyEnglishLab for more skill practice.

CONNECT THE READINGS

ORGANIZE

Use the information in the readings to complete Dr. Perry's chart.

> **USE YOUR NOTES**
>
> Use your notes from Reading One and the information from Reading Two to complete the chart.

	Ann	Elisa	Rosa	Sam	Ali
Name of Phobia					
The Fear of					
Effect / Results					

SYNTHESIZE

1 Imagine you are Dr. Perry. Continue the chart from the Organize section. Write suggestions for each person.

	Ann	Elisa	Rosa	Sam	Ali
Suggestions	-Read about spiders -Look at photos of spiders -Try to relax when you see a spider -Talk about your fear of spiders	Read about snakes Look at photos of snakes	-Try to relax when you see a high place -Talk about your fear of high places	-Look at photos of needles -Talk about your fear of needles	

2 Work with a partner. Student 1: You are Elisa, Rosa, Sam, or Ali. Talk about your fear. Student 2: You are Dr. Perry. Give suggestions to Student 1. Then switch roles. Take turns talking about a fear and giving suggestions. Use information from the charts in the Organize and Synthesize sections.

Student 1: Dr. Perry, I have a phobia of _____ . Because of my fear,
_____

Student 2: I understand. I have some advice. _____
_____

Student 1: Thanks for your help, Dr. Perry. I will try your ideas.

Go to **MyEnglishLab** to check what you learned.

3 FOCUS ON WRITING

VOCABULARY

REVIEW

Complete the paragraphs by unscrambling the words in parentheses.

Experts say that anyone can have a (pahibo) _____1._____ . A (nlmrao) _____2._____ person like you or me can have a fear. Even a famous person like Jackie Chan can have a fear.

Jackie Chan is a movie star from Hong Kong. In his movies, Jackie does dangerous things. For example, he may fall from a tall building. In real life, Jackie Chan is (arfdia) _____3._____ of something. He has a fear of (nedesle) _____4._____ .

Many people have this fear. These people (aswte) _____5._____ when they see a needle. They (pnica) _____6._____ at the doctor's office. They (viaod) _____7._____ doctors. It is difficult for them to feel (raelxde) _____8._____ . They think the idea of a needle is (ugdsgtsini) _____9._____ .

If you think you have a phobia, talk about your (frae) _____10._____ with friends or family. Don't feel (erambrssade) _____11._____ . You are not alone.

What Are You Afraid Of? 107

EXPAND

ADJECTIVES + PREPOSITIONS

We can use some adjectives alone or with specific prepositions. These prepositions connect the adjectives to other words in the sentence.

Examples

I saw the spider, and I was afraid.

I am afraid of spiders.

> NOT: *I am afraid about spiders.*

I felt embarrassed when my family laughed.

I am embarrassed about my phobia.

> NOT: *I am embarrassed of my phobia.*

Study the list of adjective + preposition combinations.

afraid of	happy about	nervous about	scared of
embarrassed about	interested in	relaxed about	

Read the sentences. Circle the correct preposition.

1. Jackie Chan is afraid (of / about) needles.
2. I'm happy (of / about) your advice.
3. I am interested (about / in) phobias.
4. Ann never feels relaxed (of / about) spiders.
5. A person with acrophobia feels nervous (of / about) high places.
6. Ali is scared (of / in) public speaking.
7. You shouldn't be embarrassed (about / of) your fear.
8. Some people are afraid (of / in) dogs.

CREATE

APPLY Write five sentences that are true for you. Use five adjectives from the box and the correct prepositions.

| afraid | embarrassed | happy | interested | nervous | relaxed |

Example

I am interested in reading books.

1. _____
2. _____
3. _____
4. _____
5. _____

Go to the **Pearson Practice English App** or **MyEnglishLab** for more vocabulary practice.

GRAMMAR FOR WRITING

1 On *askdoctorperry.com,* Dr. Perry chats with people who need help. Max is a person who has a problem. Read part of their online conversation. Pay attention to the boldfaced words. Underline the verbs. Then study the charts below.

MAX: **Can** you help me? My friend asked me to visit his house. But I **can't** go to my friend's house. I'm scared.

DR. PERRY: Why are you scared?

MAX: I'm afraid of cats. I **can't** go to my friend's house because he has a cat. The cat **may** hurt me.

DR. PERRY: I **can** help you. Tell me, is the cat mean? Did it hurt you in the past?

MAX: No, the cat isn't mean. But I'm afraid.

DR. PERRY: You **might** have a phobia. First, call your friend. Tell him about your fear. He **will** understand.

MAX: OK, but I still feel scared.

DR. PERRY: Read about cats. You **may** feel less scared.

2 Look again at the boldfaced words in Exercise 1. What form of verb comes after each boldfaced word?

Modals: Can, May, Might, and Will	
1. *Can, may, might,* and *will* are **modals**. Always use the **base form of the verb** after modals.	[base form] I **can help** you. [base form] The cat **may hurt** me. [base form] You **might have** a phobia. [base form] He **will understand**.
2. The negative of modals is **modal + *not***. Always use **the base form of the verb** after **modal + *not***.	[base form] The cat **cannot hurt** you. [base form] The cat **may not hurt** you. [base form] The cat **might not hurt** you. [base form] The cat **will not hurt** you.
3. Use *cannot* for *can + not*.	[base form] He **cannot understand** my fear.
4. Use *won't* for *will + not* in speaking and informal writing.	[base form] The cat **won't hurt** you.
5. Use *can't* in speaking and informal writing.	[base form] I **can't go** to my friend's house because he has a cat.
6. A modal changes the meaning of the verb that follows. *Can* often means **ability**. *May* and *might* often mean **possibility**. *Will* means a **future prediction**.	 I **can** help you. I **can't** go to my friend's house. You **may** feel less scared. You **might** have a phobia. He **will** understand.

3 Read Dr. Perry's online chat with Kate. Complete each sentence with the correct modal and the verb in parentheses.

1. Use *can / can't*.

   KATE: Dr. Perry, I need help. I'm afraid of public speaking. But in my English class next week, I need to do a presentation. I _____ in front of the other
   (speak)
   students. I _____ of correct words, and I _____ at
   (think)   (look)
   the class. I'm scared!

   DR. PERRY: I _____ you. Don't worry, Kate. You _____ a good
   (help)   (give)
   presentation.

2. Use *may / might* or *may not / might not*.

   KATE: Really?

   DR. PERRY: Yes. Many people have a fear of public speaking. Other students in your class
   _____ afraid, too.
   (feel)

   KATE: I didn't think of that. You _____ right. That's good news!
   (be)

   DR. PERRY: Of course! Public speaking is hard, so the presentation _____
   (be)
   easy. But that is normal.

3. Use *will / will not / won't*.

   KATE: OK. But everyone _____ at me when I speak.
   (look)

   DR. PERRY: They are your friends. They _____ at you. They want you to feel
   (laugh)
   relaxed, so they _____ politely.
   (listen)

   KATE: I hope so. I _____ about your advice!
   (think)

4 Phillip and his wife are going to Jamaica for vacation. Phillip is afraid of flying in airplanes. Choose the answers that complete Phillip's sentences.

1. On our vacation, flying in an airplane _____ be scary.
   (will / can)

2. I _____ panic in the airplane.
   (can / may)

3. Other people _____ laugh at me.
   (might / can)

4. Sometimes when I'm afraid, I _____ think clearly.
   (won't / can't)

5. My wife is not scared. She _____ fly with no problem.
   (can / might)

What Are You Afraid Of?

5 APPLY **Write five suggestions for Phillip, affirmative or negative. Use four different modals. Then share your sentences with the class.**

1. _____
2. _____
3. _____
4. _____
5. _____

6 There are seven mistakes in the sentences. Find and correct six more mistakes.

1. A doctor can ~~to~~ help you.
2. Isabelle has a phobia of needles, so she no can go to the doctor.
3. Lisa may has a phobia of spiders.
4. She no will go in the attic, and she can't sleeping.
5. I might be have a phobia.
6. You may afraid of snakes.

Go to the **Pearson Practice English App** or **MyEnglishLab** for more grammar practice. Check what you learned in **MyEnglishLab**.

FINAL WRITING TASK: Suggestions APPLY

In this unit, you read about people who have phobias. Some people have phobias, but all people feel afraid of something.

You are going to ***write a response giving suggestions*** to someone who is afraid. Use the vocabulary and grammar from the unit.

For an alternative writing topic, see page 117.

PREPARE TO WRITE: Brainstorming

Read the blog post from someone who wants help.

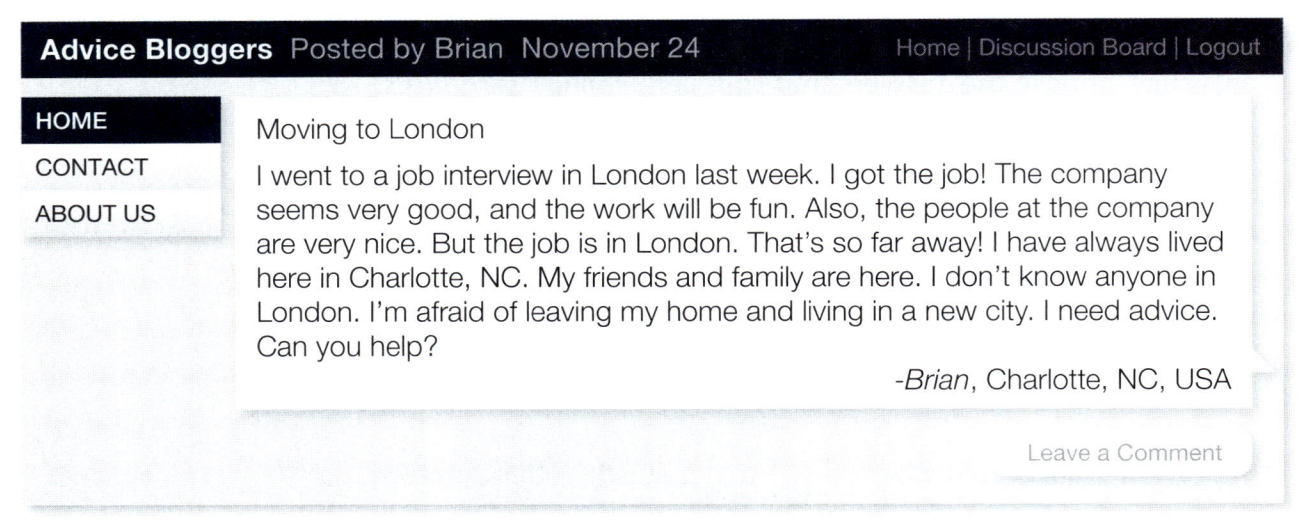

Advice Bloggers Posted by Brian November 24   Home | Discussion Board | Logout

HOME
CONTACT
ABOUT US

Moving to London

I went to a job interview in London last week. I got the job! The company seems very good, and the work will be fun. Also, the people at the company are very nice. But the job is in London. That's so far away! I have always lived here in Charlotte, NC. My friends and family are here. I don't know anyone in London. I'm afraid of leaving my home and living in a new city. I need advice. Can you help?

-*Brian*, Charlotte, NC, USA

Leave a Comment

1 Respond to Brian. To help you plan this response, work with a partner and answer the questions. Then complete the Suggestions column in the chart.

How can Brian feel better? What can he do?

Suggestions	Brian will feel better because . . .
• Brian can chat with his family online.	• He won't feel alone.
•	•
•	•
•	•

2 Look again at your list. Say more about each idea. You might ask yourself, "Why will this help Brian?" or "How will this idea make Brian feel better?" Write your answers in the chart under Brian will feel better because . . .

3 Choose 2 or 3 ideas that are best or most interesting. You can use these ideas in your message to Brian.

WRITE: Make Suggestions

When you make a suggestion, follow these steps:

1. Show that you understand the problem.
2. Give your suggestion.
3. Give a reason for your suggestion.
4. Conclude by offering help or a final comment.

1 Donna lives in Perth, Australia. Read Donna's message to an online group.

Advice Bloggers   Home | Discussion Board | Logout

HOME
CONTACT
ABOUT US

I work for a great company. I give personal attention to customers. I like speaking to one customer at a time, and customers like me. Last week, my boss offered me a better job at the company. I will make more money, and I will teach employees about giving personal attention. But I will have to speak to large groups of employees. I'm afraid of public speaking! I always panic and sweat. What can I do?

—*Donna*, Perth, Australia

Leave a Comment

What Are You Afraid Of?

2 Read the sentences. Think about the steps to make suggestions above. Put the sentences in order. Then compare your answers with a partner's.

____ When you practice at home, you will get better at public speaking.

__1__ I was afraid of talking to groups, too, so I think I understand your situation.

____ A class might help you relax in front of a group.

__2__ You can take a class for public speaking.

____ Also, you can practice at home every day.

____ I'm sure you'll be great at your new job. Good luck!

3 Use the sentences in Exercise 2 to write a response to Donna. Then compare your response with a partner's.

Dear Donna,

_____
_____
_____
_____
_____
_____
_____

4 Now write the first draft of your response to Brian. Use the steps for making suggestions to help you.

REVISE

ADDING SUPPORTING DETAILS

Supporting details help to explain your ideas and make your writing more interesting. When you write, think about these questions:

- *Why is this idea important?*
- *How can I help my reader understand more easily what I mean?*
- *What examples can I give to make my idea clearer?*
- *What else can I write to make this more interesting?*

Asking these questions can help you add supporting details to your writing.

1 Read the question (Q) and the answer (A). In the answer, underline the suggestions once. Underline the supporting details twice. The first one has been done for you.

> Q: My friend is having a big party with a lot of people. I don't like parties! Being around a lot of people makes me nervous. I'm scared of talking to new people. I don't know what to talk about. Sometimes I panic. What can I do?
> —Mary, Dublin, Ireland
>
> A: I think I understand your problem. Talking with new people scares me, too. <u>Just try to be friendly at the party.</u> <u>Smile and say hello.</u> You can also write a list of ideas to talk about. Think about your list at the party. It will help you have something to talk about. I always do this, and it helps. I know what to talk about, so I feel more relaxed. You might want to tell your friend how you feel before the party. And remember, there may be others who are afraid, too. Sometimes you can be more relaxed because someone else knows how you feel. You might even have some fun. It is a party! Good luck!

2 Write supporting details to complete the answer. Then share your response with a partner.

> A: I can understand how you feel. I feel nervous with new people, too. You can go to the party with a person you know. _____
>
> _____
>
> _____
>
> Also, you might go home after one or two hours. _____
>
> _____
>
> _____
>
> Good luck at the party!

3 Now look at the first draft of your response to Brian. What supporting details can you add? Make changes as needed.

Go to **MyEnglishLab** for more skill practice.

What Are You Afraid Of? **115**

EDIT: Writing the Final Draft

APPLY Write the final draft of your response. Check your grammar, spelling, capitalization, and punctuation. Be sure to use some of the grammar and vocabulary from the unit. Use the checklist to help you write your final draft.

FINAL DRAFT CHECKLIST

- ☐ Did you give suggestions to Brian?
- ☐ Did you begin with a good topic sentence?
- ☐ Did you use supporting details?
- ☐ Did you use basic modals (*can*, *will*, *may*, and *might*)?
- ☐ Did you use vocabulary from the unit?

ALTERNATIVE WRITING TOPIC

APPLY Not everyone has a phobia, but everyone has a fear. Write a paragraph about something you are afraid of. When did your fear start? Why? What can you do to feel better? Use vocabulary and grammar from the unit.

_____
_____
_____
_____

CHECK WHAT YOU'VE LEARNED

Check (✔) the outcomes you've met and vocabulary you've learned. Put an X next to the skills and vocabulary you still need to practice.

Learning Outcomes
- ☐ Infer meaning
- ☐ Note definitions
- ☐ Identify causes and effects
- ☐ Use basic modals (*can, may, will, might*)
- ☐ Add supporting details
- ☐ Write suggestions

Vocabulary
- ☐ afraid (of)
- ☐ avoid
- ☐ disgusting
- ☐ embarrassed (about)
- ☐ fear
- ☐ happy (about)
- ☐ interested (in)
- ☐ needles
- ☐ nervous (about)
- ☐ normal AWL
- ☐ panic
- ☐ phobia
- ☐ relaxed (about) AWL
- ☐ scared (of)
- ☐ sweat

Go to **MyEnglishLab** to watch a video about weird phobias, access the Unit Project, and take the Unit 5 Achievement Test.

LEARNING OUTCOMES

> Make inferences about people
> Take notes with a timeline
> Separate fact from opinion
> Use the simple past
> Use time order words
> Write a narrative paragraph

Go to **MyEnglishLab** to check what you know.

UNIT 6

What an Adventure!

1 FOCUS ON THE TOPIC

1. What is the Spirit of St. Louis?
2. Do you know the man in the picture? If yes, who is he? If not, what do you think he did?

2 FOCUS ON READING

READING ONE | Lindbergh Did It!

VOCABULARY

1 Read the list of words and their definitions.

adventure: an exciting thing that someone does or that happens to someone

contest: a game that people try to win; a competition

flight: a trip in an airplane

hero: someone you respect very much for doing something good

landed: arrived somewhere in an airplane (past form of *land*)

media: (plural) newspapers, magazines, radio, and television

pilot: the person who flies an airplane

set a record: did something faster or better than ever before (past form of *set a record*)

solo: alone, with no other people

took off: left a place in an airplane (past form of *take off*)

unforgettable: not possible to forget

2 Read about Lindbergh's trip on the *Spirit of St. Louis.* Complete the sentences with words from the list.

  In 1919, Raymond Orteig started a _____*contest*_____ . He offered $25,000 to the first
                    1.

pilot to fly non-stop across the Atlantic Ocean between New York and Paris. In 1927, Charles

Lindbergh was the winner of the contest.

  In the 1920s, flying airplanes was a new science. Charles Lindbergh, a young airmail

_____ , was very interested in flying. When he learned about Orteig's contest,
   2.

he decided to enter it. He was ready for this great _____ . And he wanted to fly
                    3.

_____—just himself.
   4.

  On May 10, 1927, Lindbergh _____ from San Diego, California. He stopped in
                5.

St. Louis, Missouri, for gas and oil. Then he quickly continued on to New York.

(continued on next page)

He _____ in New York on May 12th. His trip from San Diego to New York
        6.
was less than 22 hours. He _____ for the fastest _____ across
                           7.   8.
the United States.

This was only the beginning of Lindbergh's historic trip. Lindbergh was on his way to
becoming an international _____ . People from the _____ ,
                          9.   10.
—newspapers, magazines, and radio, followed him from that day until the end of his life. For
Lindbergh and people around the world, this was a(n) _____ experience.
                                                      11.

 Go to the **Pearson Practice English App** or **MyEnglishLab** for more vocabulary practice.

PREVIEW

You are going to read a newspaper article about Charles Lindbergh. At first, people called Lindbergh "The Flying Fool[1]." Why do you think they called him this? Check (✓) the answers you think are correct.

_____ The weather was bad.

_____ Lindbergh was too young to fly.

_____ The plane was too small to cross the ocean.

_____ Lindbergh was not a good student in school.

_____ The trip was too long.

_____ Your ideas: _____

---
[1] A "fool" is someone who people think is stupid or crazy.

What an Adventure! 121

READ

Read the newspaper story. Create a chart like the one below to take notes. On the left, put the main ideas. On the right, put the details.

TAKE NOTES

Main Ideas	Details	
• Charles Lindbergh	• handsome	•
•	• flew solo from NY to France	•

Go to **MyEnglishLab** to view example notes.

LINDBERGH DID IT!

By Jacques Moreau, *Paris Express News* Staff Writer **Paris Express News—May 27, 1927**

1 PARIS, FRANCE—One week ago, Charles Lindbergh was just a handsome, 25-year-old airmail **pilot** from a small town in the United States. Today, he is the most famous man in the world and the most important man in the history of flying.

2 Last week, Lindbergh started out on an **adventure**. He flew **solo** from New York to France. He was the first person to fly non-stop across the Atlantic Ocean alone. He also **set the record** for the longest non-stop **flight**.

3 Lindbergh **took off** on his historic flight on May 20th at 7:52 a.m. People called him "The Flying Fool." On that day, other pilots in the **contest** waited in New York because the weather was very bad. Lindbergh decided not to wait. He took five sandwiches, a bottle of water, a notebook, a pen, and a compass. He didn't even have a radio. All he heard was the sound of the wind and the noise from the plane's engine. He was in the air all alone with his thoughts, his hopes, and his fears.

4 After 3,610 miles, 33 hours and 30 minutes and no sleep, Lindbergh **landed** in Paris on May 21st. At that moment, his life changed forever. There were 150,000 excited people waiting to greet him. The international **media** were also there. Photographers and newspaper reporters wanted to be the first to tell Lindbergh's story. When he got out of his plane and saw all the excitement, he knew that his life would never be the same again.

5 When he began this **unforgettable** flight, he was a quiet young man from a quiet town. This morning, "Lucky Lindy" left Paris as an international **hero**.

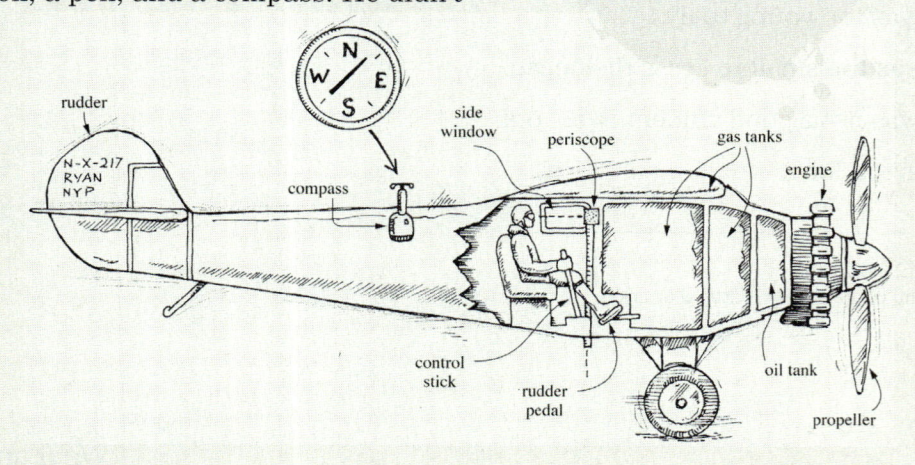

MAIN IDEAS

Circle the best answer to complete each statement.

1. In 1927, Lindbergh set the record for the _____ non-stop flight.
   a. first
   b. longest
   c. highest

2. He was the first person to fly non-stop from _____ .
   a. France to the United States
   b. The United States to France
   c. New York to San Diego

3. The people waiting in Paris were very _____ .
   a. excited
   b. quiet
   c. confused

4. Because of his historic flight, Lindbergh became very _____ .
   a. handsome
   b. lucky
   c. famous

DETAILS

1 Use one of the numbers from the box to answer each question. Write your answers in complete sentences.

| 150,000 | 3,610 | 7:52 | one | the 21st |
| ~~25~~ | 33½ | five | the 20th | |

1. How old was Lindbergh when he flew across the Atlantic?

   <u>Lindbergh was 25 years old when he flew across the Atlantic.</u>

2. On what date did he take off from New York?

   _____

3. At what time in the morning did he take off from New York?

   _____

4. How many people were on Lindbergh's plane when he flew across the Atlantic?

   _____

5. How many miles was Lindbergh's flight?

   _____

6. For how many hours was he in the air?

   _____

7. How many sandwiches did he take on his trip?

   _____

8. On what date did he land in Paris?

   _____

9. About how many people greeted him when he arrived in Paris?

   _____

2 **APPLY** Look at your notes and at your answers for Main Ideas and Details. How did your notes help you complete the exercises?

MAKE INFERENCES

Making Inferences about People

An **inference** is an **educated guess** about something. The information is **not stated directly** in the reading. Good readers put ideas together to find the right answer. You can use what you already know and what you read in the text to understand more about a person in the reading.

We can understand what kind of person Charles Lindbergh was by thinking about his actions and his words. We also learn about Lindbergh from what other people (here, the writer) said about him.

Example

Was Charles Lindbergh an adventurous person (someone who likes excitement or adventures)?

From paragraph 3, we know that Lindbergh entered Orteig's contest, and he flew across the Atlantic in bad weather. He took off when other pilots stayed on the ground. He also flew alone. From this information, we can infer that Charles Lindbergh was adventurous.

Look at the reading again and at the list of adjectives below. Do you think they describe Charles Lindbergh? Work with a partner. Ask and answer the question. Explain your answer by pointing to ideas in the reading.

Was he _____ ?

Adjectives

- determined (having a strong desire to do something)
- independent (liking to be alone, not needing other people)
- simple (not complicated)
- social (liking talking with people)
- competitive (wanting to be the best at something)

Yes, he was. I think he was _____ .

   In paragraph #_____ , it says _____ .

No, he wasn't. I don't think he was _____ .

   In paragraph #_____ , it says _____ .

DISCUSS

Do you think Lindbergh was nervous before or after his flight? Find information in Reading One to support your answers. Explain your answers to a partner.

1. I think (don't think) he was nervous *before* his flight because _____ .

2. I think (don't think) he was nervous *after* his flight because _____ .

> **USE YOUR NOTES**
>
> Use your notes to support your answers with information from the reading.

Go to **MyEnglishLab** to give your opinion about another question.

READING TWO | Crash Landing on the Hudson River

PREVIEW

1. Look at the title of the reading and the pictures. Write two questions that you think will be answered in this reading.

   _____

   _____

2. Look at the boldfaced words in the reading. Which words do you already know? What does each word mean?

READ

1 Read about this unforgettable adventure. As you read, guess the meaning of the words that are new to you. Remember to take notes on main ideas and details.

Crash Landing on the Hudson River

New York Daily Post — By Sally Martínez Staff Writer

1 On January 15, 2009, U.S. Airways flight 1549 took off from LaGuardia Airport in New York City at 3:24 p.m. It was going to Charlotte, North Carolina. There were 150 passengers and five crew members on board—the pilot, the co-pilot, and three flight attendants. The flight seemed like any trip, but very quickly it became an unforgettable adventure.

2 Unfortunately, three minutes after take-off, a flock of birds hit the plane's engines. First, the left engine was on fire and stopped working. Then the second engine also stopped.

3 Captain Chesley "Sully" Sullenberger, the pilot, had to make a fast decision. He did not have enough time to fly back to LaGuardia. He had to do something. If he did nothing, then everyone on the plane was going to die, including himself. At 3:31 p.m., Sullenberger decided to land on the Hudson River. "We're going to be in the Hudson," he told the airport. It was very **risky**, but he had to try. He used his experience as a pilot and as a glider[1] pilot to land the airplane on the Hudson River. As a result, all of the people on the plane lived.

4 The next day, people called this **event** the "Miracle[2] on the Hudson." They couldn't believe it was possible to land such a big plane on a river. Passengers on the plane were very thankful to Sullenberger. One passenger told reporters, "Captain Sullenberger is the best pilot in the world." Another said, "He is a great leader! He should be the President of the United States."

5 U.S. government officials will study this unforgettable event. They do not want it to happen again. For now, people are just happy to be alive. Everyone agrees: It was an adventure they do not want to repeat.

---
[1] **glider:** a very light plane with no engine
[2] **miracle:** something amazing that happens that you thought was impossible; in some religions, something only God can make happen

2 Compare your notes on main ideas and details with a partner's. How can you improve your notes next time?

Go to the **Pearson Practice English App** or **MyEnglishLab** for more vocabulary practice.

NOTE-TAKING SKILL

Taking Notes with a Timeline

When you take notes, use a timeline to show time order. A timeline shows events in time order. With a timeline, you can easily review and retell a story.

To make a timeline, follow these steps:

Read the story, and think: What happened? When?
Draw a line across the page.
Write the first event (with the date or time) on the left side, and write the last event on the right side.
Complete the timeline. Write the other events in time order, working from left to right (earliest to latest).

Tips:

If you have specific times or dates, space events evenly on the timeline. For example, ½ inch (1 cm.) can show one year or one day. One minute will have a smaller space.

Do not write sentences. Just use important words.

Example:

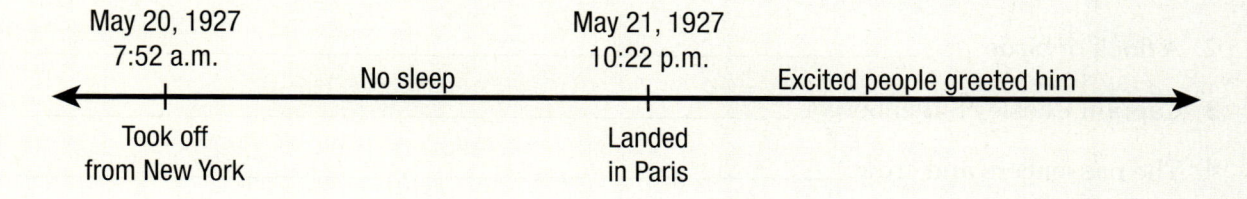

```
May 20, 1927                    May 21, 1927
7:52 a.m.                       10:22 p.m.
      ←———————No sleep—————————————|————Excited people greeted him————→
      Took off                  Landed
      from New York             in Paris
```

1 Make a timeline using the information below. Draw a line from the time to the event. Then make a timeline of the events.

Times:	Events:
5:00 a.m.	Drove to the airport
5:30 a.m.	Got back on the plane to do it again
6:30 a.m.	Got on the plane
7:00 a.m.	Got out of bed
7:01 a.m.	Jumped out of the plane with a parachute
7:06 a.m.	Landed on the ground
8:00 a.m.	Opened the parachute

```
5:00 a.m.
    ←———|————————————————————————————————→
     Got out
     of bed
```

What an Adventure! **127**

2 Look at Reading Two again. Make a timeline of events in the story "Crash Landing on the Hudson River." Write the events on the lines.

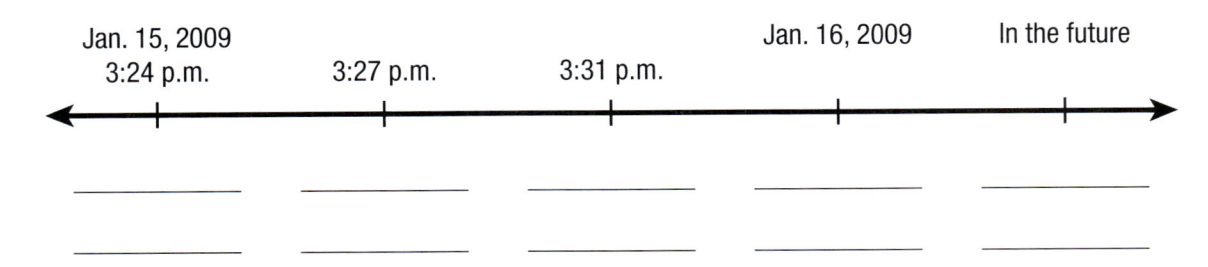

```
Jan. 15, 2009                                    Jan. 16, 2009      In the future
   3:24 p.m.       3:27 p.m.       3:31 p.m.
◄──────┼───────────────┼───────────────┼───────────────┼───────────────┼──────►
```

_____   _____   _____   _____   _____

_____   _____   _____   _____   _____

 Go to **MyEnglishLab** for more note-taking practice.

COMPREHENSION

1 Complete the sentences with information from the reading.

1. U.S. Airways Flight 1549 _____

   _____

2. A flock of birds _____

3. Captain Chesley Sullenberger _____

4. The passengers and crew _____

2 Review the boldfaced words from the reading with a partner. Use a dictionary or ask your teacher for any meanings you still do not know.

READING SKILL

1 Look at paragraph 4 of Reading Two again. Notice the information in bold. Which sentence is a fact (we know it's true)? Which is an opinion (people can agree or disagree)? Complete the chart.

> 4 **Days later, people called this event the "Miracle on the Hudson."** They couldn't believe it was possible to land such a big plane on a river. Passengers on the plane were very thankful to Sullenberger. One passenger told reporters, **"Captain Sullenberger is the best pilot in the world."** Another said, "He is a great leader! He should be the President of the United States."

Fact	Opinion

128   UNIT 6

Separate Fact from Opinion

When you read, it is important to notice the difference between facts and opinions. A fact is something that we know is true. We can check the information and agree. An opinion is a personal idea or belief. People can agree with our opinions or disagree with them.

Example

> **People called this event the "Miracle on the Hudson."**

It is a fact that people called it a miracle. We can check the news reports. People really did call it the "Miracle on the Hudson."

> **Captain Sullenberger is the best pilot in the world.**

This is an opinion. Captain Sullenberger is a very good pilot, but not everyone will agree that he is the best pilot in the world.

Note: The statement "A passenger said Captain Sullenberger is the best pilot in the world." is a fact. It is true that a passenger said this.

2 Look at Reading One on page 122 again. Read each sentence. Decide if the sentence is a fact or an opinion. Write F (fact) or O (opinion).

_____ 1. Charles Lindbergh was internationally famous.

_____ 2. He set the record for the longest non-stop flight.

_____ 3. Lindbergh was a fool.

_____ 4. Lindbergh didn't take enough food on his flight.

_____ 5. On the day that Lindbergh's plan took off, the weather was bad.

_____ 6. He was very brave to fly solo across the Atlantic.

Go to **MyEnglishLab** for more skill practice.

CONNECT THE READINGS

ORGANIZE

Look at Readings One and Two again. Complete the chart. Then discuss your answers with the class.

> **USE YOUR NOTES**
>
> Use your notes from Reading One and your timelines to complete the chart.

	Beginning How did his adventure begin?	**Middle** What problems did he have?	**End** How did his adventure end?
Charles Lindbergh			
Chesley Sullenberger			

SYNTHESIZE

Charles Lindbergh and Chesley Sullenberger lived in different times. Both of them had a big adventure that made them famous. Use information from the chart in the Organize section to finish the summary of their adventures.

Charles Lindbergh and Chesley Sullenberger were both pilots, and they both had big adventures.

On May 20, 1927, Charles Lindbergh _____ . People thought he was a fool because _____ . Also, he _____ . However, after 33 hours, _____ . Everyone was amazed! Lindbergh was famous! Many years later, on January 15, 2009, Captain Sullenberger _____ . Very soon, he had a big problem: _____ . The plane _____ . Everyone was amazed when Captain Sullenberger _____ and _____ . People said he was a hero.

⬆ Go to **MyEnglishLab** to check what you learned.

130 UNIT 6

3 FOCUS ON WRITING

VOCABULARY

REVIEW

Read the story about Amelia Earhart. Choose the words that complete the sentences.

Amelia Earhart (1897–1937) was a ___pilot___ .
1. (pilot / writer)
She became interested in flying while working in Canada during World War I. She started flying in 1922.

In 1928, Earhart _____ across the
2. (flew / flight)
Atlantic Ocean. She was the first woman to do this, but on this flight Earhart was not the pilot. She was only a passenger. This _____ made her very
3. (flight / contest)
famous. She was a _____ to many women
4. (pilot / hero)
and girls. People called her "Lady Lindy."

Then, in 1932, she _____ another record. She became the first woman to fly
5. (set / flew)
solo across the Atlantic. She —_____ from Harbour Grace, Newfoundland, and
6. (took off / landed)
_____ near Londonderry, Ireland. In 1935, she became the first person to fly solo
7. (took off / landed)
from Hawaii to California.

In 1937, Earhart and another pilot, Fred Noonan, decided to fly around the world. This flight was _____ , but the danger did not stop Earhart. She wanted more
8. (lucky / risky)
_____ .
9. (adventures / events)
Sadly, their plane was lost in the Pacific Ocean. No one knows exactly what happened to them. It's a mystery. Even today there are stories in the _____ about Amelia
10. (media / adventures)
Earhart and her mysterious last flight.

Today people still read about Earhart's life. For them, her story is _____ .
11. (lucky / unforgettable)

What an Adventure! 131

EXPAND

USING SYNONYMS

A *synonym* is a word that has a similar meaning to another word. Use synonyms to make your writing more interesting.

The **price** of the *Spirit of St. Louis* was $10,580.
The **cost** of the *Spirit of St. Louis* was $10,580.

The plane was **built** in San Diego, California.
The plane was **constructed** in San Diego, California.

Read each sentence. Change the underlined word to a synonym from Reading One on page 122 and Reading Two on page 126. Follow the example.

1. Lindbergh departed from New York on May 20, 1927. *took off*

2. The *Spirit of St. Louis* arrived in France on May 21, 1927.

3. He flew across the Atlantic alone.

4. Lindbergh won the competition that Orteig started in 1919.

5. The press gave Lindbergh a lot of attention in the newspapers and on the radio.

6. Lindbergh became well known all over the world.

7. His historic trip changed his life.

8. Amelia Earhart was another famous flier.

9. Sullenberger had to make a very fast choice.

10. Trying to land an airplane on a river was very dangerous.

CREATE

APPLY Imagine that you were a passenger on Captain Sullenberger's flight. Write a paragraph in your diary about that unforgettable event. What happened? How did you feel? Write at least five sentences. Use words from the unit.

Friday, January 16th

Yesterday was a day that I will never forget. I really can't believe what happened. First,

___

___

___

___

Go to the **Pearson Practice English App** or **MyEnglishLab** for more vocabulary practice.

GRAMMAR FOR WRITING

1 Read the paragraph. Notice the boldfaced simple past verbs. Then answer the questions.

> On March 1, 1932, someone **kidnapped** Charles and Anne Lindbergh's baby. The kidnapper **left** a note in the baby's bedroom. In the note, the kidnapper **asked** for $50,000. Lindbergh **paid** the money. Unfortunately, on May 12, 1932, someone **found** the baby. He **was** dead. In 1935, the police **arrested** Bruno Richard Hauptmann. Hauptmann **said**, "I **didn't do** it!" Many people **did not believe** him. The court **decided** that he **did** it. As a result, Hauptmann **died** in the electric chair[1] on April 2, 1936. Today, some people believe that Hauptmann **did not kidnap** the Lindbergh baby.
>
> [1] **electric chair:** a chair that uses electricity to kill people as a punishment for a crime

1. Which past tense verbs are regular? Make a list.
2. Which past tense verbs are irregular? Make a list.
3. How do you form the simple past in negative sentences for regular verbs?

The Simple Past	
1. Use the **simple past** to talk about actions completed in the past.	People *called* Lindbergh "The Flying Fool."
2. To form the simple past:	**Base Form** **Simple Past**
For **regular verbs,** add *-ed* to the **base form.**	land land**ed** return return**ed**
If the base form ends in *-e,* add only *-d.*	receive receive**d** live live**d** die die**d**
If the base form ends in a consonant followed by *-y,* change the *-y* to *-i* and add *-ed.*	marry marr**ied** try tr**ied**
If the base form ends with consonant-vowel-consonant, double the last consonant, then add *-ed.*	kidnap kidnap**ped** stop stop**ped**
3. Many verbs have irregular past forms.	become **became** buy **bought** do **did** fly **flew** go **went** make **made** take **took** think **thought**
4. To make **negative statements,** use: *didn't* (*did not*) + the base form	Lindbergh *didn't have* a radio with him.
5. To ask *wh-* questions, use: *Wh-* word + *did* + subject + the base form **Note:** If you do not know the subject of the question, do not use *did.*	When *did* Earhart *disappear?* [subject] Who *kidnapped* the Lindberghs' baby? What *happened* to the Lindberghs' baby?

What an Adventure!

2 Complete the paragraphs with the simple past form of the verbs.

Raymond Orteig _____started_____ the flying contest for two reasons. First, Orteig
                    1. (start)
_____ to build friendship between the United States and France. He also
   2. (want)
_____ it _____ important for people to have an interest in
   3. (think)   4. (be)
flying. Five pilots _____ to cross the Atlantic during the 1920s, but they
                         5. (try)
_____ successful. The flight _____ very risky. Six men
   6. (not / be)   7. (be)
_____ trying to win the contest. Finally, Lindbergh _____ it. After
   8. (die)   9. (do)
Lindbergh _____ in Paris, people _____ him a hero. Later, he
             10. (arrive)   11. (call)
_____ one of the most famous men in the world.
   12. (become)

Lindbergh _____ very independent. He _____ strong
                13. (be)   14. (have)
opinions. For example, he _____ the United States to enter World War II.
                              15. (not / want)
He _____ that Germany _____ too strong. Many people
      16. (believe)   17. (be)
_____ with his opinions. At that time, they _____ Lindbergh
   18. (not / agree)   19. (not / think)
_____ a hero at all.
   20. (be)

3 APPLY Write questions about Charles Lindbergh. Write three *yes / no* questions and three *Wh-* questions in the simple past. Then share your questions with the class.

   Example
   Did Charles and Anne Lindbergh have any children?
   Was Charles Lindbergh a fool?

1. _____
2. _____
3. _____

   Example
   Why did Lindbergh enter Orteig's contest?

4. _____
5. _____
6. _____

Go to the **Pearson Practice English App** or **MyEnglishLab** for more grammar practice. Check what you learned in **MyEnglishLab**.

FINAL WRITING TASK: A Narrative Paragraph APPLY

In this unit, you read about Charles Lindbergh and his first solo, non-stop flight across the Atlantic Ocean. You also read about Captain Chesley "Sully" Sullenberger, who safely landed his plane on the Hudson River and saved the lives of the people on board.

You are going to *write a narrative paragraph about a trip or adventure.* You can write about your own experience or that of another person. Use the vocabulary and grammar from this unit.

For an alternative writing topic, see page 141.

PREPARE TO WRITE: Brainstorming

To help you write about your trip or adventure, you are going to **brainstorm ideas.** When you brainstorm, you think of as many ideas as possible. Then you make a list of your ideas.

1 **Brainstorm a list of trips or adventures you had. Think of experiences with your family, friends, or classmates. Then think about *Wh-* and *yes / no* questions for more ideas on that topic.**

   Examples

   - Drove my father's car without asking and had an accident
     - Where did I go?
     - Was the car expensive?
     - Who was there?
     - Was anyone hurt?
     - What did my father say?
   - Took a road trip across the United States with friends
   - Went hiking in the mountains and got lost
   - Lost my wallet while traveling
   - Went skydiving for the first time

2 **Think about the experience you chose in Exercise 1. Add more details to the chart on page 141 to help you write later.**

   Example

   Took a road trip across the United States with friends / saw many fun things / car broke down[1]

Wh- Questions	Notes
Who?	Jenny, Lisa, Jackie—my classmates
When?	Three years ago
Where?	Visited cities, states, and national parks across the United States—driving east to west and then back
Why?	We wanted adventure. It was our dream to do it.
How?	In Lisa's car
How many?	Three people, 10 states
How much?	Cheap hotels, expensive to fix the car

---

[1] **broke down:** stopped working

What an Adventure!

Wh- Questions	Notes
Who?	
What?	
When?	
Where?	
Why?	
How?	
How many?	
How much?	

Note: You don't have to answer every question when brainstorming.

WRITE: A Narrative Paragraph

A **narrative** is a story about an event or experience. The writer tells the story in time order starting with the first event and ending with the last event.

1 Read the sentences. Then put them in order. Number them from 2 to 8.

On Saturday, I went dancing with my friends. . . .

_____ At 12:00 a.m., I said good night to my friends, and I walked to the Metro.

_____ At 7:00 a.m., the Metro opened again. I got on. This time I did not fall asleep.

_____ I got on the train, I sat down, and I fell asleep. I was so tired from dancing.

_____ I left the train, and I walked out of the Metro. I was totally lost!

_____ Then I looked at my watch. It was after 3:00 a.m. No more trains!

__1__ We danced for three hours.

_____ When I woke up, someone was saying, "Get up! Last Stop!"

_____ I had no money for a taxi, so I went to a 24-hour coffee shop to wait for the Metro to open.

2 Now write the sentences in paragraph form in your notebook. Be sure to indent your paragraph.

3 Look at the timeline and complete the paragraph. Use past verb forms.

Our Weekend in Toronto

←FRIDAY	SATURDAY	SUNDAY	MONDAY→
• fly from Philadelphia to Toronto • take a nap • visit with family / friends at night	• walk around the city • lose wallet and passport • spend rest of day trying to get them back	• buy gifts for friends • have special dinner to celebrate our trip • pack our suitcases	• get home

Last year, my friend and I took a weekend trip to Canada. On Friday, we _____ . When we arrived at the hotel, we _____ . Later that day we
  1.   2.
_____ . On Saturday, we woke up early and _____ . Unfortunately,
  3.   4.
I _____ . We _____ . It was very frustrating. Then on Sunday, we
     5.   6.
_____ . That night, we _____ . Finally, we _____ . We
  7.   8.   9.
_____ home late Monday evening.
  10.

4 Now write the first draft of your narrative paragraph about your trip or adventurous experience. Think about your answers to the *Wh-* questions in Prepare to Write, Exercise 2.

REVISE

Time order words show the order of events in a narrative. They help your reader understand your story.

Using Time Order Words

Time order words often come at the beginning of a sentence.

Example

I went to the beach with my brothers last week. **First,** we just sat on the beach. **Then** we went swimming in the ocean. **Next,** we played football in the sand. **Finally,** after three hours, we went home.

Other time words or expressions tell when or how long:

A specific day
On Wednesday, we flew to Boston. (*on Tuesday, on Friday, on Saturday*)

In the past
Last year, I went to London. (*last week, last month, yesterday*)
I went to Sydney **two years ago.** (*two months ago, two weeks ago, two days ago*)

(continued on next page)

In the future
We left **the next day**. (*the next week, the next month, the next year*)
We arrived in Florida on **Tuesday. Five days later,** we went to Georgia. (*three hours later, a year later*)

A period of time
We went to Florida **for a week**. (*for an hour, for a month, for a year*)

Note: Use time order words and expressions to make your writing clear for your reader. Don't use them in every sentence.

1 Look back at the paragraph about the trip to Toronto in Write, Exercise 3, on page 137. Underline the time order words or other time words.

2 Read the timeline below. Then choose the time expression that best completes each sentence. Write the correct time expression on the line.

Monday, June 6	-Left Washington, D.C. -Drove towards Las Vegas, Nevada -Stopped in Bedford, Pennsylvania
Monday, June 13	-Arrived in Las Vegas
Tuesday, June 14	-Left Las Vegas -Drove towards Flagstaff, Arizona -Car broke down 10 miles before Flagstaff
Wednesday, June 15	-Stayed in Flagstaff
Thursday, June 16	-The Grand Canyon
Friday, June 17	-Flagstaff
Sunday, June 19	-Left Flagstaff
Tuesday, June 21	-Arrived back in Washington, D.C.

THE ROAD TRIP

_____*Three years ago*_____, my friends and I drove across the United States. It was an
1. (Three years ago / First)

unforgettable adventure. _____, June 6th, we left Washington, D.C. and
2. (For a week / On Monday)

drove west towards Las Vegas, Nevada. We drove _____. While driving,
3. (five years later / for six days)

we stopped at many beautiful small towns, big cities, and national parks, but we got very tired

of driving. _____, on Monday, June 13th, we arrived at Las Vegas,
4. (Finally / First)

Nevada. This was our last stop going west. We walked around the streets and looked at all the

lights and people. _____, on Tuesday, we began driving east again.
5. (The next day / The day before)

_____ something terrible happened. Our car broke down near Flagstaff,
6. (Then / Finally)

Arizona. Flagstaff was not in our plans, but we stayed there _____.
7. (two days ago / for five days)

Flagstaff is a nice town with many nice restaurants, cafés, and used bookstores. What a

surprise! We took small trips near Flagstaff, including the Grand Canyon. It was amazing!

_____, our car was ready. We quickly drove back to D.C. We arrived
8. (Five days ago / Five days later)

back home in D.C. _____.
9. (on Tuesday / two months ago)

3 Now look at the first draft of your narrative paragraph. Underline the time order words.
Is the order of events clear? Add or change time order words if needed.

Go to **MyEnglishLab** for more skill practice.

EDIT: Writing the Final Draft

APPLY Write the final draft of your paragraph. Check your grammar, spelling, capitalization, and punctuation. Be sure to use some of the grammar and vocabulary from the unit. Use the checklist to help you write your final draft.

FINAL DRAFT CHECKLIST

- ☐ Did you write a narrative paragraph?
- ☐ Did you begin with a good topic sentence?
- ☐ Did you use vocabulary from the unit?
- ☐ Did you use simple past verbs?
- ☐ Did you put your ideas in a time order?
- ☐ Did you use time order words and expressions?

ALTERNATIVE WRITING TOPIC

APPLY Interview someone you know about a trip or adventure he or she had. Write a narrative paragraph about the experience. Use vocabulary and grammar from the unit.

_____
_____
_____
_____
_____

CHECK WHAT YOU'VE LEARNED

Check (✔) the outcomes you've met and vocabulary you've learned. Put an X next to the skills and vocabulary you still need to practice.

Learning Outcomes
- ☐ Make inferences about people
- ☐ Take notes with a timeline
- ☐ Separate fact from opinion
- ☐ Use the simple past
- ☐ Use time order words
- ☐ Write a narrative paragraph

Vocabulary
- ☐ adventure
- ☐ arrive
- ☐ build
- ☐ choice
- ☐ contest
- ☐ competition
- ☐ construct AWL
- ☐ cost
- ☐ dangerous
- ☐ decision
- ☐ depart
- ☐ event
- ☐ famous
- ☐ flight
- ☐ flier
- ☐ hero
- ☐ land (v.)
- ☐ media AWL
- ☐ pilot
- ☐ press (n.)
- ☐ price
- ☐ risky
- ☐ solo
- ☐ trip
- ☐ unforgettable

Multi-word Units
- ☐ set a record
- ☐ took off
- ☐ well known

Go to **MyEnglishLab** to watch a video about a heroic pilot, access the Unit Project, and take the Unit 6 Achievement Test.

LEARNING OUTCOMES

> Infer comparisons
> Take notes with a tree diagram
> Recognize and understand pronoun reference
> Use comparative adjectives
> Use connecting words
> Write a comparison paragraph

Go to **MyEnglishLab** to check what you know.

What Number Are You?

UNIT 7

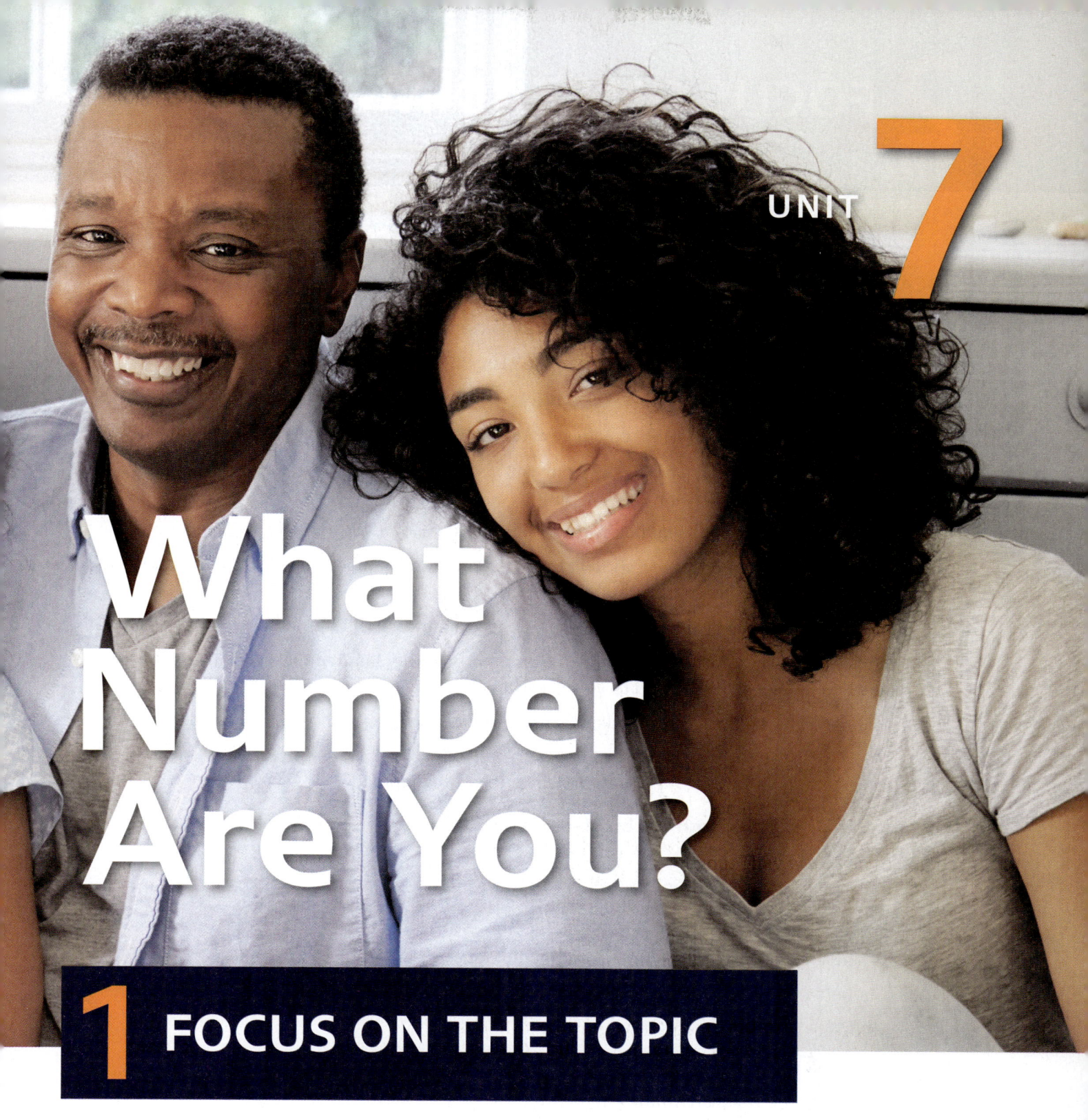

1 FOCUS ON THE TOPIC

1. How many brothers and sisters are there in this family?
2. What is a good number of brothers and sisters to have?

2 FOCUS ON READING

READING ONE | Timing Is Everything

VOCABULARY

1 Read the sentences. Pay attention to the boldfaced words.

1. My friend Kam has ten **siblings.** He is the 11th child in his family.
2. David studied hard for the test. He is **likely** to do well on it.
3. My parents **expect** me to go to college after high school, but I want to travel for a year.
4. My little sister is really **spoiled.** My parents give her everything she wants. She never says thank you. She just wants more and more.
5. Even "good" kids **misbehave** sometimes. No child is good all the time.
6. People say all tall people are good at basketball, but that's just a **stereotype.** I'm tall, but I am not good at basketball.
7. My parents had many **rules.** One was to do my homework right after school.
8. When I was young, my parents were very **strict** with me. I had to go home after school to do my homework. Also, I had to go to bed at 8:00 p.m.
9. In my family, there are three kids. My sister is the oldest, I am the **middle** child, and my brother is the youngest.
10. Polly was **born** in Boston, but she now lives in Philadelphia.

2 Match the definitions with the boldfaced words above. Write the number of the sentence on the line.

_____ probably, almost certainly

_____ brothers and sisters

_____ behaving badly because you get too much money or attention, or too many things

_____ in between two people or things

_____ starting life, coming out of your mother's body

_____ to think something will or should happen in the future

_____ making sure rules are followed

_____ to behave or act badly

_____ an idea about a particular type of person which is wrong or unfair

_____ instructions about what you can and cannot do

⟶ Go to the **Pearson Practice English App** or **MyEnglishLab** for more vocabulary practice.

144 UNIT 7

PREVIEW

Read this paragraph about John Isaacs. Then decide if he is the oldest, middle, or youngest child in his family. Choose one. Explain your answer to a partner.

John Isaacs is a medical doctor in Chicago. He is very successful and respected in the community. He is married and has two children. They live in a nice house. His parents live nearby. John sees his parents often and gives them money every month. They go on vacations with John and his family.

I think John Issacs is probably the _____ child in his family because
(oldest / middle / youngest)
_____ .

READ

Read a section from a textbook about families. Create a chart like the one below to take notes. On the left, put the main ideas. On the right, put the details.

Main Ideas	Details
1. The First Born	• very responsible
2.	
3.	

Go to **MyEnglishLab** to view example notes.

What Number Are You? 145

TIMING IS EVERYTHING

1. Members of the same family have similarities. However, research shows that there are differences among oldest, **middle**, and youngest children. Scientists want to know: What are the differences and where do they come from?

The First Born

2. Oldest children are often very responsible[1] and organized. The reason is the parents. Parents **expect** the oldest child to be an example for the younger children to follow.

3. **First-born** children are often more educated than younger **siblings**. As a result, firstborns are more **likely** to have high-paying jobs. They become CEOs and doctors.

4. Firstborns get a lot of attention from their parents at an early age. However, they also have more **rules** to follow than younger children. For example, they have an early bedtime. New parents are usually **stricter** with their first child.

The Middle Child

5. Middle children do not have the benefits of the oldest child. They also do not have the freedom of the youngest. Unlike the oldest and youngest, middle children are never alone in the family. They have to share their parents' time, attention, or money with other siblings.

6. Middle children have to work harder to get attention. Sometimes they feel left out, so they **misbehave** to get attention. They are called the "problem children." Also, they might look outside the family to get attention or to feel special.

7. Middle children are often independent. They are good at solving[2] problems. They can get help from the oldest, but they can also help the youngest. However, middle children often go to their friends for advice, not to their parents or siblings.

The Baby

8. When the third child arrives, parents are usually more confident[3] but less energetic than before. As a result, the youngest child often has more freedom. Bedtimes are later. Parents are also more generous with their money. The baby usually gets what he or she wants. This is a problem if the child becomes **spoiled**.

9. Last-born children are often more adventurous. They are more likely to take risks. They play risky sports such as ice hockey or football. The youngest is also more likely to be an artist, a firefighter, or an independent business owner.

10. They are also funny. When you are the little one, older siblings will be nice to you if you make them laugh.

11. Some people think that parents cause the personality differences in their children. Other people say these birth order descriptions are not true; they are just **stereotypes**. Of course, every family is different. However, studying birth order may help us understand families.

---

[1] **responsible:** behaving in a sensible way and can be trusted
[2] **solving:** finding the answer
[3] **confident:** feeling sure that you can do something well

MAIN IDEAS

Read each sentence. Choose the main idea in the reading. Put a check (✓).

_____ 1. People agree that birth order stereotypes are true.

_____ 2. There is a connection between birth order and personality.

_____ 3. Birth order differences come only from the parents.

DETAILS

1 According to the reading, do these words and phrases describe the first-born (1), middle (2), or last-born (3) child in a family? Write the number on the line.

_____ adventurous   _____ funny   _____ left out

_____ oldest   _____ organized   _____ the "problem" child

_____ the problem solver _____ responsible   _____ spoiled

_____ youngest   _____ more educated   _____ independent

2 Look at your notes and your answers from the Preview section. How did they help you understand the text?

MAKE INFERENCES 🔍

Inferring Comparisons

An **inference** is an **educated guess** about something. The information is **not stated directly** in the reading.

Writers often make **comparisons**—show how two things are the same or different. Sometimes these comparisons are not always directly stated. You have to make inferences to understand the comparisons.

A comparison sentence usually mentions the two people or things in the comparison.

   #1   #2
First-born children are often **more educated than** younger siblings. (paragraph 3)

A writer may not always mention the second person or thing.

   #1
First-born children are often **more educated.**

In this sentence the reader infers **than younger siblings.**

Can you infer the second part of this example?

 New parents are usually **strict** with their first child. (paragraph 4)

You can infer that the writer is comparing first-born children with younger children. Here is the sentence with both parts:

                  #1   #2
 New parents are usually **stricter** with their first-born child **than with their younger children.**

Answer each question with a comparison. Use the boldfaced words in your answers. Look at the paragraphs in parentheses. Answers may vary.

1. Who has **higher-paying jobs**? (paragraph 3)

   <u>Firstborn children have higher-paying jobs than their younger siblings.</u>

2. Who has to **work harder to get attention**? (paragraph 6)

   _____

3. Who is **more adventurous**? (paragraph 9)

   _____

4. Who is **more likely to be a firefighter**? (paragraph 9)

   _____

DISCUSS 🔍

Read your notes from Reading One again. Then think about the first-born, middle-born, or last-born children in a family you know. Does the research on birth order seem true to you? Complete the statements to answer the question and explain why.

> **USE YOUR NOTES**
>
> Use your notes to support your answers with information from the reading.

Example

I don't think the research on last-born children is true. My friend Nan is the youngest. She is responsible. She is not spoiled.

1. I think the research on _____ -born children is true.
   (first / middle / last)

   _____

2. I'm not so sure the research on _____ -born children is true.
   (first / middle / last)

   _____

3. I don't think the research on _____ -born children is true.
   (first / middle / last)

   _____

Go to **MyEnglishLab** to give your opinion about another question.

READING TWO | Case Study: The Koh Family

PREVIEW

1. Reading Two is about a family with three siblings who are all adults. Write two questions that you think will be answered in this reading.

   _____
   _____
   _____

2. Look at the boldfaced words in the reading. Which words do you already know? What does each one mean?

READ

1. A case study is a long, descriptive example. Read this case study from a sociology textbook. As you read, notice the boldfaced words. Try to guess the meaning from the context. Remember to take notes on main ideas and details.

CASE STUDY: THE KOH FAMILY

1. Vincent and Helen Koh live in Arcadia, California. They have three children. They are all **adults** now.

2. Ellen, the oldest, lives in Arcadia. In fact, Ellen and her parents are next-door **neighbors**. Unfortunately, she does not see her parents often. She is the busy mother of three daughters. She is the CEO of the Arcadia Savings Bank. She also volunteers twice a week at the local hospital. These are only three of her responsibilities.

3. The Koh's middle child, Tim, lives in Los Angeles, about an hour away from his parents. He visits often and helps them with their computer problems. Tim is married to Sally. Their son, Steven, is in high school.

4. Tim stays home and takes care of his family. He works part-time selling houses. Tim loves risky sports. He plays ice hockey once a week. Tim, his wife, and his son go skiing almost every weekend in the winter.

5. Jeff is the youngest. He is the "baby," but he is almost 40 years old. He lives in Philadelphia, far away from his parents. Jeff got his PhD in biology, and he is now a university professor. Like his sister, he also volunteers at a hospital. On weekends, he performs[1] in a comedy club. He enjoys it. When he was young, he always made his family laugh. Now people pay him to be funny.

[1] **perform**: to do something to entertain people

2. Compare your notes on main ideas and details with a partner's. How can you improve your notes next time?

⬆ Go to the **Pearson Practice English App** or **MyEnglishLab** for more vocabulary practice.

What Number Are You? 149

NOTE-TAKING SKILL

Drawing a Tree Diagram

When you take notes, use a tree diagram to show relationships. A family tree is a type of tree diagram. It shows the relationship among family members.

Look at the family tree of the British royal family.

British Royal Family

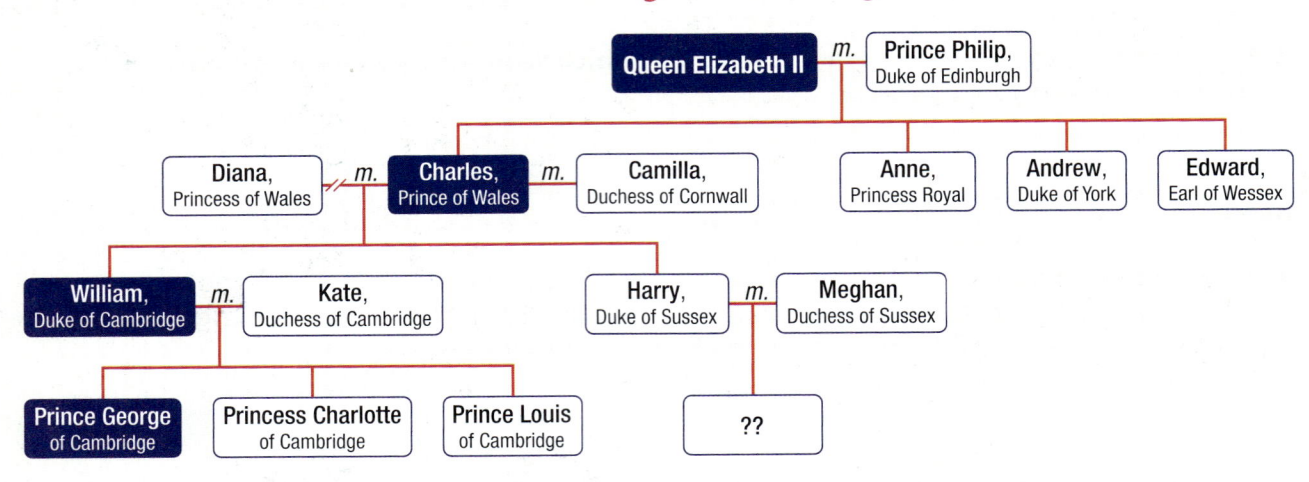

```
                    Queen Elizabeth II —m.— Prince Philip, Duke of Edinburgh
                            |
   ┌────────────────────────┼────────────────┬─────────────┬──────────────┐
Diana,       Charles,     Camilla,        Anne,          Andrew,       Edward,
Princess —m.— Prince  —m.— Duchess of     Princess Royal Duke of York  Earl of Wessex
of Wales    of Wales      Cornwall
   |
   ├─────────────────────────┐
William, —m.— Kate,          Harry, —m.— Meghan,
Duke of     Duchess of       Duke of     Duchess of
Cambridge   Cambridge        Sussex      Sussex
   |                            |
┌──┼─────────┐                  |
Prince    Princess    Prince     ??
George    Charlotte   Louis
of        of          of
Cambridge Cambridge   Cambridge
```

Here's how you make a tree diagram:

1. Start with the oldest or most senior person or people on top.

2. Put people from one group or generation on the same line or level. For example, put brothers and sisters on the same level.

3. Put the next group on the next level. For example, put children under their parents.

4. On a family tree, if a person gets married more than one time, show that with "m." as you see in the tree diagram above.

1 Choose one.

　　a. Draw your own family tree. Start with your grandparents, or before, if you can.

　　b. Draw the organizational chart of a sports team or group you belong to.

　　c. Draw the organizational chart of the place where you work.

2 Look at Reading Two again. Draw the Koh's family tree.

🔁 Go to **MyEnglishLab** for more note-taking practice.

COMPREHENSION

1 Read each statement. Write T (true) or F (false). If the statement is false, change one word to make it true.

_____ 1. Vincent and Helen Koh have 4 grandchildren.

_____ 2. Ellen is a CEO at a hospital.

_____ 3. Tim lives with his family in Philadelphia.

_____ 4. Tim enjoys sports.

_____ 5. Jeff is the first-born child in this family.

2 Review the boldfaced words from the reading with a partner. Use a dictionary or ask your teacher for any meanings you still do not know.

READING SKILL

1 Look at Reading Two again. Then read the sentences. Choose the word or phrase from the box that means the same as the underlined word.

| Ellen's | doing stand-up comedy | Tim and Sally's |
| Tim, Sally, and Steve | ~~Vincent and Helen Koh~~ | being a parent, a CEO, and a volunteer |

1. They have three adult children. (paragraph 1) Vincent and Helen Koh

2. Ellen and her parents are next-door neighbors. (paragraph 2)
_____

3. These are only three of her responsibilities. (paragraph 2)
_____

4. Their son, Steven, is in high school. (paragraph 3)
_____

5. They all go skiing almost every weekend in the winter. (paragraph 3)
_____

6. He enjoys it. (paragraph 4)
_____

Understanding Pronoun Reference

A noun names a person, place, thing, or idea. A pronoun is a word that takes the place of a noun.

When you read, it is important to connect pronouns to the correct noun. Understanding these connections can help you understand what you read.

Sometimes the pronoun refers to a noun in the same sentence. Other times the pronoun refers to a noun in an earlier sentence.

Subject pronouns: *I, you, he, she, it, we, they*

Example
They have three adult children. (*They* refers to *Vincent and Helen Koh*.)
They all go skiing almost every weekend in the winter. (*They* refers to *Tim, Sally, and Steve*.)

Object pronouns: *me, you, him, her, it, us, them*

Example
He enjoys it. (*It* refers to *performing stand-up comedy*.)

There is also a connection between nouns and possessive adjectives (*my, your, his, her, its, our, their*)

Example
Ellen and her parents are next-door neighbors. (*Her* refers to *Ellen*.)
Their son, Steven, is in high school. (*Their* refers to *Tim and Sally*.)

The words *this, that, these,* and *those* are demonstrative pronouns. They make connections to ideas stated before.

Example
These are only three of her responsibilities. (*These* refers to *being a parent, a CEO, and a volunteer*.)

2 Look at Reading One on page 146 again. Then read the sentences. Write the word or phrase that means the same as the underlined word. Use the paragraph numbers in parentheses to help you find the information.

1. This is because parents have high expectations. (paragraph 2)

   being responsible and organized

2. They become CEOs and doctors. (paragraph 3)

   _____

3. New parents are usually strict with their first-born children. (paragraph 4)

   _____

4. Middle children may go to their friends for advice, not their parents. (paragraph 7)

   _____

5. The "baby" usually gets what he or she wants. (paragraph 8)

   _____

6. This is a problem if the child becomes spoiled. (paragraph 8)

   _____

7. <u>They</u> play risky sports like ice hockey or rugby. (paragraph 9)

_____

8. Others see some truth in <u>them</u>. (paragraph 11)

_____

Go to **MyEnglishLab** for more skill practice.

CONNECT THE READINGS

ORGANIZE

Review the information of birth order in Reading One and the descriptions of the Koh children in Reading Two. Complete the chart. Then compare your answers with a partner.

USE YOUR NOTES

Use your notes from Reading One and the information from Reading Two to complete the chart.

Ideas from Reading One	Ideas from Reading Two	
	Typical	Not Typical
The First Born • responsible • organized • educated	Ellen is the oldest. She is very responsible and organized. She is a CEO of a bank. I think she went to college.	Ellen . . .
The Middle Child • independent • looks outside the family for attention • the "problem child" • the problem solver		
The Baby • adventurous • artistic • funny • spoiled		

What Number Are You?

SYNTHESIZE

Think about how the Koh children fit (or do not fit) the ideas in Reading One. Use the chart from the previous page. Then complete the sentences.

1. _____ doesn't really fit the description of a _____-born child.
   (Name)   (first / middle / last)

   _____ is a problem solver. But _____ isn't the "problem child." Also,
   (She / He)   (She / He)

   _____ thinks about family a lot. _____ also enjoys adventurous
   (She / He)   (She / He)

   sports. _____ is more adventurous than the other siblings.
           (She / He)

2. _____ fits the description of a _____-born child. _____
   (Name)   (first / middle / last)   (She / He)

   has a very high-paying job. _____ is very responsible. As a bank CEO,
                               (She / He)

   _____ also has a higher-paying job than the other siblings.
   (She / He)

3. _____ partly fits the description of a _____-born child.
   (Name)   (first / middle / last)

   _____ isn't spoiled or adventurous. But _____ is very funny.
   (She / He)   (She / He)

   _____ is funnier than the other siblings.
   (She / He)

Go to **MyEnglishLab** to check what you learned.

3 FOCUS ON WRITING

VOCABULARY

REVIEW

Complete the passage with the correct word from the box.

| adults | confident | likely | misbehave | rules | stereotypes |
| born | ~~expect~~ | middle | neighbor | spoiled | strict |

The Only-Child Syndrome

An only child is a person with no siblings. Some people think only children are selfish, lonely, or unhappy. They say it is difficult for an only child to play or work with others. This is called the "Only-Child Syndrome."

It is true that parents ___expect___ a lot from their only child—similar to the oldest child
                           1.
in other families. Only-children are often very responsible. They are also better at communicating because they speak mostly with _____ at home.
                                      2.

Like _____ children, only children are more _____ to make friends
      3.   4.
outside the home. This is natural. They need to play with other kids.

Like the youngest children, only children may be a little _____ by their parents.
                                                           5.
They get 100 percent of their parents' time and attention.

Some parents are _____—their children have to follow a lot of _____.
                  6.   7.
But no child is good all the time. All children _____ sometimes.
                                                 8.

Polly Hollingsworth is my next-door _____. We were also _____ on
                                      9.   10.
the same day. She is also an only child. Polly says that she was not lonely or unhappy. She doesn't fit the description of an only child. Today, Polly is very _____. She can talk to people
                                                                  11.
easily, and she is not afraid of anything.

Spoiled? Lonely? Unhappy? These may be _____. There is no big difference
                                         12.
between only children and people with siblings. Only children are just like other children.

What Number Are You?   155

EXPAND

Read the idioms and expressions about families. Then complete the sentences with an idiom or expression about family. Use the correct form of the verb.

sibling rivalry: competition between brothers and sisters in a family

the black sheep: the family member who has a different life from the others

raise a family / children: care for and give your children the things they need. Parents raise a family. They raise their children.

grow up: get older. Children grow up and become adults.

take after: be similar to an older family member, such as a parent or sibling

It runs in the family: All the family members have something in common, such as hair color or personality.

1. Everyone in my family went to college. They all work in offices, and they all live in the city. I decided not to go to college. I live on a farm. I am definitely _____ of the family.

2. Jane's father is a great tennis player. Jane plays tennis well, too. Jane _____ her father.

3. Mr. and Mrs. Sullivan were very friendly to their neighbors. Their children are friendly, too. Friendliness _____ .

4. Patrick and Peter are twins. There is a lot of _____ between them. One is always trying to be better than the other in school and in sports.

5. You need a lot of money to _____ . You need to pay for clothes, food, and school.

6. Raymond doesn't want to _____ . He wants to be a teenager forever.

CREATE

APPLY In your notebook, write six sentences about your family. Use the words and phrases from the Review and Expand sections.

Go to the **Pearson Practice English App** or **MyEnglishLab** for more vocabulary practice.

GRAMMAR FOR WRITING

1 Molly and Holly are sisters. Read the chart. Then circle the correct answers.

	Molly	**Holly**
Young	is 25 years old	is 24 years old
Tall	is 5'2" tall (157 cm.)	is 5'7" tall (170 cm.)
Friendly	is friendly	is a little shy
Athletic	was in the Olympics once	watched the Olympics on TV once

1. Which sister is younger, Molly or Holly?
   a. Holly is younger than Molly.
   b. Molly is younger than Holly.

2. Which sister is taller?
   a. Holly is taller than Molly.
   b. Molly is taller than Holly.

3. Who is friendlier?
   a. Holly is friendlier than Molly.
   b. Molly is friendlier than Holly.

4. Which one is more athletic?
   a. Holly is more athletic than Molly.
   b. Molly is more athletic than Holly.

Comparative Adjectives

1. Use the comparative form of adjectives to compare two people, places, or things. Use **than** when you are comparing two things in a sentence.	Holly is **taller than** her sister Molly. Molly is **more athletic than** Holly.
2. For adjectives with one syllable, add **-er + than**. cool smart old short shy strict tall young Notice the spelling change for adjectives that end in consonant-vowel-consonant: big → bigger thin → thinner	Molly is **shorter than** Holly. Holly is **younger than** Molly. Sydney is a big city. Tokyo is **bigger than** Sydney. Molly is **thinner than** Holly.
3. For adjectives with two or more syllables, use **more + adjective + than**. adventurous athletic boring exciting handsome interesting	Molly is **more intelligent than** Polly.
4. For adjectives with **two syllables** that end in **-y**, change the **-y** to **-i** and add **-er + than**. busy friendly funny risky heavy lucky wealthy	Molly is **friendlier than** Holly.

(continued on next page)

5. Some adjectives have irregular comparative forms. bad → **worse** *than* fun → **more fun** *than* good → **better** *than* likely → **more likely** *than* quiet → **quieter** *than* spoiled → **more spoiled** *than*	Holly is a **goo**d cook. Holly is a **better** cook **than** Molly (is).

2 Phil and Bill are brothers. Study the chart. Pay attention to how they are similar and different.

Phil	Bill
is 38 years old	is 40 years old
is 5' 10" (178 cm)	is 6' (183 cm)
is average looking	is handsome
is a brain surgeon	is a teacher
works 14 hours a day	works 10 hours a day
makes $500,000 a year	makes $50,000 a year
drives a new Ferrari	drives an old Hyundai
enjoys watching TV	enjoys traveling and climbing mountains

3 Look at the information about Phil and Bill. Complete all the questions. Use the correct comparative form of the word in parentheses. Then answer the questions.

1. Which brother is _____*taller*_____ (tall)?   _____Bill is taller than Phil._____

2. Which one is __*more handsome*__ (handsome)?   Bill is more handsome than Phil.

3. Which one is _____ (good-looking)?   _____

4. Which brother drives a _____ (cool) car?   _____

5. Who is _____ (old)?   _____

6. Which brother is _____ (busy)?   _____

7. Which one is _____ (adventurous)?   _____

8. Which brother is _____ (interesting)?   _____

9. Which one has a _____ (exciting) life?   _____

10. Which is probably _____ (fun) to go on a date with?   _____

4 **APPLY** Both Phil and Bill asked Jill on a date. She needs to choose. Which brother should Jill go out on a date with? Why? Write five sentences. Use comparative adjectives.

Jill should go out on a date with _____ because . . .
                                   (Phil / Bill)

_____

_____

_____

_____

Go to the **Pearson Practice English App** or **MyEnglishLab** for more grammar practice. Check what you learned in **MyEnglishLab**.

FINAL WRITING TASK: A Comparison Paragraph APPLY

In this unit, you read about stereotypes about birth order. You also read about the members of the Koh family.

You are going to ***write a comparison paragraph about two family members.*** They can be members of your family or another family. You will write about how they are similar or different. Use the vocabulary and grammar from the unit.

For an alternative writing topic, see page 165.

PREPARE TO WRITE: Using a Venn diagram

A Venn diagram helps you think about the similarities and differences between two things. In the center, you can list all the similarities. On the two sides, you can list the differences. The Venn diagram on page 160 describes Prince William and Prince Harry, pictured here.

The Venn diagram makes it easy to see the similarities and differences between the two brothers.

1 Look at the information about Ellen and Tim. Then complete the Venn diagram.

Prince William Differences
- was born in 1982
- is 6'3" (190.5 cm)
- is 2nd in line to be king
- has many royal responsibilities

Similarities
- are the sons of Prince Charles and Princess Diana
- are married
- enjoy sports
- live in England

Prince Harry Differences
- was born in 1984
- is 6'1 (185 cm)
- is 6th in line to be king
- has some royal responsibilities

Ellen
- has a full-time job
- thinks family is important
- has three daughters
- takes them to soccer and dance
- spends time with them on weekends
- eats out with them

Tim
- has a part-time job
- thinks family is important
- has one son and wife
- runs and skis with his family
- spends time with his family on weekends
- cooks and eats at home

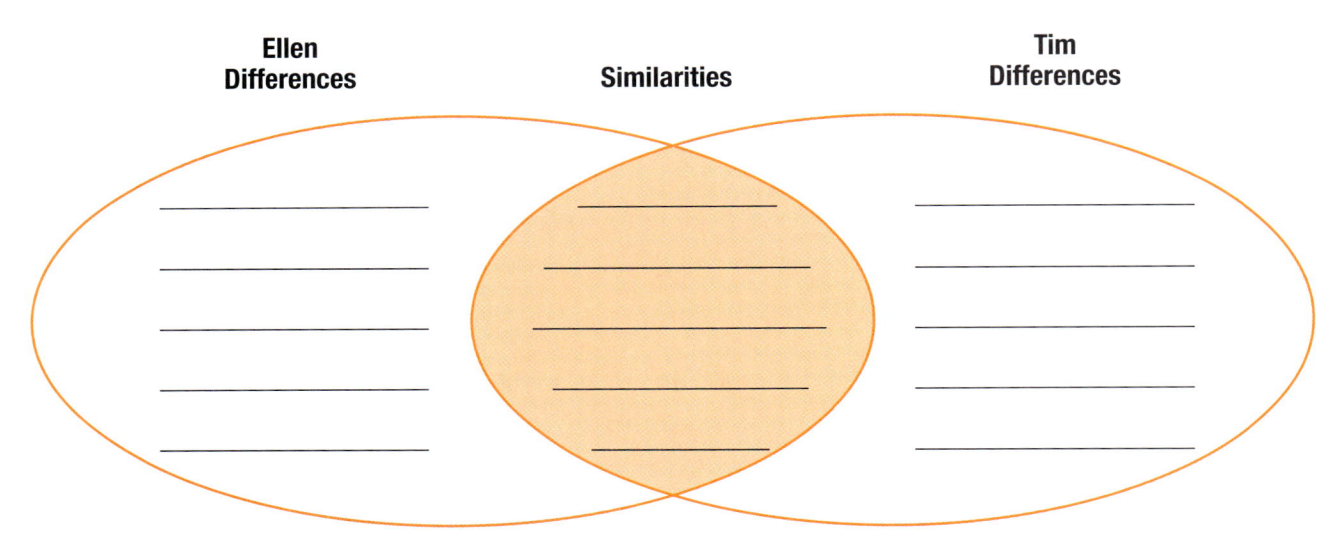

Ellen Differences   **Similarities**   **Tim Differences**

_____   _____   _____
_____   _____   _____
_____   _____   _____
_____   _____   _____
_____   _____   _____

2 Draw a Venn diagram in your notebook that shows the similarities and differences between the two people you are going to write about.

WRITE: A Comparison Paragraph

A comparison paragraph shows the similarities and / or differences between two things. It uses examples to give the reader a clear picture of the similarities and / or differences. Like other paragraphs, a comparison paragraph begins with a topic sentence. In a comparison paragraph, the topic sentence shows the purpose, or focus, of the comparison. It expresses the main idea of the paragraph. It tells the reader if the paragraph is about the similarities, differences, or both.

The body sentences give examples and details to show the similarities and / or differences. These details focus on specific points of comparison between the two things or people.

Example

> Ellen and Tim are siblings, but their weekly routines[1] are very different. Ellen has a full-time job. After work and on weekends, Ellen watches her daughters' soccer games or takes them to dance lessons. Ellen and her daughters often eat out during the week. On Saturday nights, they also like to make popcorn and watch movies. Unlike Ellen, Tim only works part-time, so he spends time with his son every afternoon. They like to run together. Every weekend they do things together. For example, they go skiing or play sports. Similar to Ellen, Tim has dinner with his family every night. He cooks, and they eat together at home. Ellen and Tim are very busy, but they spend their time in different ways.
> _____
> [1] **routines:** regular way of doing things

The main idea of this paragraph is that Ellen and Tim do different things with their families. In this paragraph, the writer makes a block comparison between Ellen and Tim. First, he decides what he wants to compare—his points of comparison: their *work* and *activities*. Then he writes about each point of comparison—first about Ellen and then about Tim. The writer concludes the paragraph by returning to the main idea of the paragraph.

1 Read the paragraph about Ellen and Tim again. Then look at the words and phrases in the box. Complete the outline. Fill in the topic sentence and the points of comparison. Use the words in the box.

activities	cooking and eating at home
eating out	full-time job
part-time job	running and skiing
taking the kids to soccer and dance	watching movies and having popcorn
work	

Topic sentence: _____

A. Ellen

    1. Work _____

    2. Activities

        a. _____

        b. _____

        c. _____

B. Tim

1. _____
2. _____
   a. _____
   b. _____

2 Work with a partner. Look at the topic sentence below, and then look at the Venn diagram about Princes William and Harry on page 160. Choose two or three points of comparison. Fill in the outline for a comparison paragraph. Then complete the paragraph about Princes William and Harry on your own in your notebook. Use the topic sentence below to begin your paragraph.

Topic sentence: *Princes William and Harry have many similarities, but, as they get older, their lives are more different.*

A. Prince William

1. _____
2. _____
3. _____

B. Prince Harry

1. _____
2. _____
3. _____

3 Write the topic sentence of your paragraph about two family members. Be sure that it states the focus of your comparison.

4 Now write the first draft of your comparison paragraph. Start with your topic sentence. Then write sentences that give details and examples about the points you are comparing. Finish your paragraph with a concluding sentence.

REVISE: Connecting words to show similarity and difference

These words and phrases will help you connect ideas in your paragraph. Use a comma after each of these phrases.

Similarity	Difference
Similar to (name),	In contrast to (name),
Like (name),	Unlike (name),

Examples

Like Ellen, her parents live in Arcadia, California. (They all live in the same city.)
Similar to Ellen, Tim has dinner with his family every night. (They both have dinner with their families but in different ways.)

Unlike most middle children, Tim enjoys playing risky sports.
In contrast to Ellen, who works at a bank, Tim works part-time selling houses.

Note that *like* means "almost exactly the same." *Similar to* is less specific. It does not mean "the same as."

1 Look at the chart. Complete the sentences with the correct names.

	Molly	Holly	Polly
Young	is 25 years old	is 24 years old	is 24 years old
Tall	is 5'2" tall (157 cm.)	is 5'7" tall (170 cm.)	is 5'2" (157 cm)
Friendly	is friendly	is a little shy	is friendly
Athletic	was in the Olympics once	watched the Olympics on TV once	was in the Olympics twice
Busy	works 20 hours a week	works 40 hours a week and goes to school	relaxes most days

1. Like ____*Molly*____ , _____ is 5'2" tall.
2. In contrast to _____ , __*who works a lot*__ , _____ isn't very busy.
3. Unlike _____ ____*and*____ _____ , _____ is 5'7".
4. Unlike her two sisters, _____ isn't very athletic.
5. Similar to her sister Molly, _____ is friendly.

2   Write sentences about the three brothers. Use the information in the chart. Then compare your sentences with a partner.

Phil	Bill	Gil
is 38 years old	is 40 years old	is 38 years old
is 5' 10" (178 cm)	is 6' (183 cm)	is 5' 10" (178 cm)
is average looking	is handsome	is not good-looking
is a brain surgeon	is a teacher	is a CEO
works 14 hours a day	works 10 hours a day	works 12 hours a day
makes $500,000 a year	makes $50,000 a year	makes $350,000 a year
drives a new Ferrari	drives an old Hyundai	drives a 2015 Ford
enjoys watching TV	enjoys traveling and climbing mountains	enjoys rap music & poetry

1. (Like / be 5'10" tall)

   Like Phil, Gil is 5'10" tall.

2. (Similar to / make a lot of money)

   _____

3. (In contrast to / drive a cool car)

   _____

4. (Like / be . . . years old)

   _____

5. (Your idea)

   _____

3   Now look at the first draft of your paragraph. Add connecting words to show similarity and difference.

Go to **MyEnglishLab** for more skill practice.

EDIT: Writing the Final Draft

APPLY Write the final draft of your paragraph. Check your grammar, spelling, capitalization, and punctuation. Be sure to use some of the grammar and vocabulary from the unit. Use the checklist to help you write your final draft.

> **FINAL DRAFT CHECKLIST**
> ☐ Did you write a comparison paragraph about two members of a family?
> ☐ Did you use a topic sentence?
> ☐ Did you use vocabulary from the unit?
> ☐ Did you have clear points of comparison?
> ☐ Did you use correct comparative forms?
> ☐ Did you use connecting words to show similarities and differences?

ALTERNATIVE WRITING TOPIC

APPLY Do you believe the ideas about birth order are true? Write a paragraph with your opinion. Use vocabulary and grammar from the unit.

CHECK WHAT YOU'VE LEARNED

Check (✔) the outcomes you've met and vocabulary you've learned. Put an X next to the skills and vocabulary you still need to practice.

Learning Outcomes
- ☐ Infer comparisons
- ☐ Take notes with a tree diagram
- ☐ Recognize and understand pronoun reference
- ☐ Use comparative adjectives.
- ☐ Use connecting words
- ☐ Write a comparison paragraph

Vocabulary
- ☐ adults AWL
- ☐ born
- ☐ expect
- ☐ likely
- ☐ middle
- ☐ misbehave
- ☐ neighbors
- ☐ rules
- ☐ sibling
- ☐ spoiled
- ☐ stereotype
- ☐ strict

Multi-word Units
- ☐ (the) black sheep
- ☐ grow up
- ☐ it runs in the family
- ☐ raise a family / child
- ☐ sibling rivalry
- ☐ take after

▶ Go to **MyEnglishLab** to watch a video about birth order, access the Unit Project, and your health and take the Unit 7 Achievement Test.

LEARNING OUTCOMES

> Infer priorities
> Take notes with an outline
> Identify the conclusion

> Use *very*, *too*, and *enough*
> Write a concluding sentence
> Write an opinion paragraph

Go to **MyEnglishLab** to check what you know.

UNIT 8

Too Young to Go Pro?

1 FOCUS ON THE TOPIC

1. What is the best age to become a professional athlete?
2. What are the benefits of being a professional athlete?[1] What are some of the drawbacks?

---
[1] **professional athlete:** someone who is paid to play a sport

2 FOCUS ON READING

READING ONE | Ready Ronnie?

VOCABULARY

1 Read about three young athletes. Pay attention to the boldfaced words.

Most soccer fans say that Brazil's Pelé was the greatest soccer player ever. He showed his **talent** for soccer at a young age. In 1958, when he was just 17 years old, Pelé became the youngest player to win the World Cup with his team. In his career, Pelé has had to **deal with** many challenges: being an athlete, being a media star, and being a role model for kids.

In 1997, at the age of 17, Martina Hingis became the youngest #1 women's tennis player. She was a great athlete, but she was not a **mature** woman yet. Martina made some **comments** about other players. For example, in 1998, she called another tennis player "old and slow." Later, Martina was much more **responsible**. When she was 22, Hingis had **difficulties** with her legs and had to stop playing tennis. She started playing again when she was 25 but retired[1] at age 27.

Chloe Kim was an athlete long before she **graduated** from high school. She started snowboarding when she was only four years old. At the 2014 Olympics, some people said Kim was the best snowboarder in the world. But she was too young to compete. At the 2018 Olympics, Kim **earned** a gold medal. She was 17 years old. Her **coach** said, "There's no one that can ride like she can."

---

[1] **retired:** stopped working

2 Match the words on the left with the definitions on the right.

_h_ 1. talent — a. taking care of others and doing what you say you will do
___ 2. mature — b. problems
___ 3. comments — c. received money or award for doing something
___ 4. responsible — d. grown up, like an adult
___ 5. difficulties — e. finished education at a school
___ 6. earned — f. try to handle a difficulty in the correct way
___ 7. graduated — g. a person who teaches a sport
___ 8. coach — h. natural ability to do something well like art, music, or sports
___ 9. deal with — i. ideas a person says or writes about something or someone

Go to the **Pearson Practice English App** or **MyEnglishLab** for more vocabulary practice.

PREVIEW

Read the title of the newspaper article. Before you read, think about what the title might mean. What do you think you will learn about Ronnie in the article? Check (✓) your ideas.

___ 1. He is going to change his name.
___ 2. He is going to move to another country.
___ 3. He is going to become a professional baseball player.
___ 4. He is going to go to college.

READ

Read the newspaper article about a special young athlete. Create a chart like the one below to take notes. On the left, put the main ideas. On the right, put the details.

TAKE NOTES

Main Ideas	Details
School life	
Ronnie Elkhouly is a young athlete.	16 years old…
Professional life	

Go to **MyEnglishLab** to view example notes.

The Metropolitan Herald

READY Ronnie?
by Richard Grayson

IN A FEW DAYS, he will be a professional baseball player. Ronnie Elkhouly will **earn** about $600,000 per year. A well-known shoe company will pay him about $2 million to wear their shoes and clothes. That is more than most other U.S. professional baseball players earn today. But right now, Elkhouly needs to finish high school.

Ronnie Elkhouly is 16 years old, and he attends the Brock Educational Institute. Brock is a school for students with special **talents** in sports or art. Many of them, like Elkhouly, **graduate** from high school early. At Brock, Elkhouly learns about math and English. Elkhouly and the other students also learn how to **deal with** living in the spotlight.[1]

There is a whole team of teachers and **coaches** helping Elkhouly to prepare for the professional world. They gave him a job at a preschool.[2] They say that taking care of three-year-olds will teach Elkhouly to be **responsible**. He will need to be responsible in the difficult world of professional sports. His coaches talk to him about the **difficulties** of being famous. For example, sometimes the media say unkind or untrue things about athletes. "People will say that Elkhouly is not **mature**. They will talk about his family. They will say he makes too much money," says one of Elkhouly's coaches. The coaches help Elkhouly understand that he cannot get angry about these **comments**.

Elkhouly also gets support from older professional athletes, like Wayne Tothrow from the Las Vegas Rattlesnakes football team. Tothrow told Elkhouly, "Go out and have fun, but take care of yourself." Tothrow also told him to be careful. He said that people—even your family and friends—can sometimes change when you have a lot of money. "Ronnie listens. He asks questions," Tothrow said.

In a few days, life will change forever for Elkhouly. He will graduate from Brock and enter the world of professional baseball. The teachers at Brock think that 16-year-old Elkhouly is mature enough to play pro baseball. But there is no test for maturity[3] at school. The real test will begin after he graduates.

---

[1] **in the spotlight:** famous; seen or watched by the public
[2] **preschool:** a school for children under six years old
[3] **maturity:** being mature

MAIN IDEAS

Check (✓) the answer that includes the most important points in the article.

_____ 1. Ronnie's teachers and coaches give him advice about the difficulties of being a pro athlete. For example, professional athletes' families sometimes want to take their money.

_____ 2. Ronnie Elkhouly will soon become a pro baseball player. He is young, so his teachers and coaches want to prepare him for the professional world. No one thinks he is mature enough to play pro.

_____ 3. Ronnie Elkhoury will soon become a pro baseball player. He is young, but his teachers and coaches are helping him become more mature very fast. Some people thinks it's a bad idea, but his coaches are not worried about him going into the professional baseball world.

DETAILS

1 Circle the best answer to complete each statement.

1. Ronnie Elkhouly will earn _____ some older professional athletes.
   a. less than
   b. the same as
   c. more than

2. Brock is a school for _____ .
   a. professional baseball players
   b. baseball and soccer coaches
   c. talented young athletes

3. One difficulty for professional athletes is _____ .
   a. taking care of small children
   b. being in the spotlight
   c. taking tests

4. The coaches at Brock are helping Elkhouly learn to _____ .
   a. deal with people's comments
   b. earn a lot of money
   c. take care of his family

5. The coaches and teachers at Brock think that Elkhouly is _____ .
   a. too young to play professional baseball
   b. strong enough to play for the Las Vegas Rattlesnakes
   c. ready to become a professional athlete

2 Look back at your notes and your answers for Main Ideas and Details. How did your notes help you understand this information?

MAKE INFERENCES 🔍

Inferring Priorities

An **inference** is an **educated guess** about something. The information is **not stated directly** in the reading. **Priorities** are the things that are most important to a person (or group of people). Writers sometimes suggest people's priorities without directly stating them. Often, people's priorities are their reasons for doing things.

Read paragraph 1 again. What is the shoe company's priority?

    a. to make money from Elkhouly's work

    b. to give advice about being famous

    c. to say negative things about Elkhouly

    d. to help Elkhouly be careful about other people

    e. to teach Elkhouly about math and other school subjects

From paragraph 1, we know that the shoe company will pay Ronnie Elkhouly a lot of money to wear their shoes and clothes. Also, we understand that companies earn money when a famous person wears their products.

The best answer is *a*. We can infer that the shoe company's priority is to make money.

What priorities do these people (or groups of people) have? Choose what is most important for each person (or group of people). Refer to the paragraphs in parentheses.

a   1. the shoe company (paragraph 1)

____ 2. Brock coaches (paragraph 3)

____ 3. Wayne Tothrow (paragraph 4)

____ 4. Brock teachers (paragraphs 1, 2)

____ 5. the media (paragraph 3)

    a. ~~to make money from Elkhoury's work~~

    b. to give advice about being famous

    c. to say negative things about Elkhouly

    d. to help Elkhouly be careful about other people

    e. to teach Elkhouly about math and other school subjects

DISCUSS

People often have more than one priority. Some of Ronnie's priorities are *playing baseball, becoming a pro player, taking care of three-year-olds, making money,* and *finishing his education.*

USE YOUR NOTES

Use your notes to support your answers with information from the reading.

Put Ronnie's priorities in order, and discuss why you think so. Support your answers with information from Reading One. Then share your ideas with a partner.

1. I think Ronnie's first (most important) priority is _____ because _____ .
2. I think that Ronnie's second (less important) priority is _____ because _____ .
3. I think _____ is not a priority for Ronnie because _____ .

Go to **MyEnglishLab** to give your opinion about another question.

READING TWO | Evan Taschen

PREVIEW

1 Look at the title of Reading Two and the picture. Check (✓) the ideas that you think will be in the reading.

_____ He is going to finish college.

_____ He is going to stop playing basketball.

_____ He is going to become a professional basketball player.

_____ Other: _____

2 Look at the boldfaced words in the reading. Which words do you already know? What does each word mean?

Too Young to Go Pro?

READ

1 Read the interview with Evan Taschen. Remember to take notes on main ideas and details.

EVAN TASCHEN: YOUNG BASKETBALL STAR SAYS "NO" TO THE PROS

Interview by Nicola Quinn

You probably don't know Evan Taschen—not yet. But basketball coaches know him, and they think he has a lot of talent. He is a college basketball star. At 19 years old and after graduating from high school, Evan Taschen is now old enough to join a professional basketball team, but the NBA[1] will have to wait. Taschen wants to graduate from college first.

NQ: Evan, everyone expected you to join the NBA this year. Why did you decide to finish college first?

ET: Well, I planned to join the NBA as soon as I was old enough. But then I met older basketball players. They **recommended** that I stay in college.

NQ: Who did you talk to?

ET: Several basketball players. But Kwasi Rodland probably helped me the most. He is my biggest basketball hero. He's the greatest. He retired in 1990. He played pro basketball for 20 years, so he has a lot of **experience**. But, in his day, all players had to go to college before joining the NBA. Today it's different. He said college helped the players to become more mature—intellectually and physically.

NQ: But what about the money? How can you say "no" to all that money?

ET: Oh, that was really hard! On the wall in my bedroom, I had photos of all the beautiful cars I wanted to buy!

NQ: So, what happened?

ET: Kwasi helped a lot. He really taught me that money is not #1. The important things in life are family, education, and health. And I still have a lot to learn.

NQ: What exactly do you need to learn?

ET: I need to learn more about working with other people—especially with people I don't agree with.

NQ: Evan, good luck to you! Do you have a final comment for our readers?

ET: I want to be a leader like Kwasi. Thirty years from now, I want people to say "Evan Taschen was—or is—a great athlete, a great leader, and a good person," not "Evan Taschen was a great athlete with a lot of expensive cars when he was 19."

[1] **NBA:** National Basketball Association

2 Compare your notes on main ideas and details with a partner's. How can you improve your notes next time?

▶ Go to the **Pearson Practice English App** or **MyEnglishLab** for more vocabulary practice.

NOTE-TAKING SKILL

Take Notes with an Outline

Students often make an outline when they take notes. An outline can help you see the order of importance of the ideas in a text. Organizing ideas in this way helps you study and remember important information.

Read the excerpt from Reading One and study the chart.

> IN A FEW DAYS, he will be a professional baseball player. Ronnie Elkhouly will earn about $600,000 per year. A well-known shoe company will pay him about $2 million to wear their shoes and clothes. That is more than most other U.S. professional baseball players earn today. But right now, Elkhouly needs to finish high school.
>
> Ronnie Elkhouly is 16 years old, and he attends the Brock Educational Institute. Brock is a school for students with special talents in sports or art. Many of them, like Elkhouly, graduate from high school early. At Brock, Elkhouly learns about math and English. Elkhouly and the other students also learn how to deal with living in the spotlight.

When you make an outline, write only the main ideas and important details. You do not need to write every idea. Write main ideas to the left. Write important details farther to the right. Remember to use only key words. You can use letters and numbers.

Example

Title: Ready Ronnie?

A. Ronnie Elkhouly
   1. 16 years old
   2. plays baseball
   3. attends school for students with special talents

B. Pro player
   1. will finish school in a few days
   2. will make a lot of money (e.g., $600K + $2 million from shoe company)

1. Read the passage. Then make an outline of the main ideas and important details in your notebook.

Motley Is Ready for More
The Louisville Observer

Most professional football players retire by the age of 35. Cashawn Motley is different. At 40 years old, Motley is the oldest player on his football team. Motley became a professional football player at the age of 19. He joined the Louisville Foxes and never stopped playing. Some people say Motley is too old to play football. Motley is not worried. "My coach and I agree that I am still good for the team," says Motley. "I want to play for ten more years!" Ten years is a long time, but Motley is still in the game for now.

2. Look again at Reading Two on page 174. Make an outline of the main ideas and details in your notebook.

Go to MyEnglishLab for more note-taking practice.

COMPREHENSION

1. Write T (true) or F (false). Discuss your answers with a partner.

   _____ 1. Evan Taschen wants to finish college before he plays pro basketball.

   _____ 2. Kwasi Rodland thinks that college is very important.

   _____ 3. Kwasi Rodland thinks that money makes athletes happy.

   _____ 4. Evan Taschen wanted to buy lots of cars, but now he thinks cars are less important than his education.

   _____ 5. Taschen wants people to think that he is a good person.

2. Review the boldfaced words from the reading with a partner. Use a dictionary or ask your teacher for any meanings you still do not know.

READING SKILL

1. Reread the end of Reading Two on page 174. What does Evan talk about? Check (✓) all the correct answers.

   At the end of Reading Two, Evan talks about _____.

   _____ his family

   _____ his hope for the future

   _____ how he learned basketball

Identify the Conclusion

When we read the **conclusion,** we know that a reading will end soon. The conclusion might be just one sentence, several sentences, or a paragraph. It comes at the end of the reading. The conclusion closes the reading and often reviews the important ideas in the reading.

Writers do this in different ways. Usually, the writer returns to one or more of the main ideas. Then the writer makes a comment about it.

> [main idea]
> *These are the reasons that I want to finish college. I have learned an important lesson: Being a good person is more important than being a basketball star.*
>
> [comment]
> *I can play pro when I am ready.*

Some writers also give an opinion in the conclusion. Giving an opinion is another way to comment on the main idea(s).

> [opinion]
> *Some people may disagree, but <u>I am happy about my decision. I believe that other young athletes should wait, too.</u>*

Some writers may also comment on the future in the conclusion. In Reading Two, the conclusion gives Evan's hope for the future.

> [hope for the future]
> *I want to be a leader like Kwasi. <u>Thirty years from now, I want people to say "Evan Taschen was—or is—a great athlete, a great leader, and a good person," not "Evan Taschen was a great athlete with a lot of expensive cars when he was 19."</u>*

When you read, look for the conclusion. Recognizing and understanding the conclusion can help you understand the most important points in the reading.

2 **APPLY** Look at Reading One on page 170 again. Reread the conclusion (paragraph 5). What do you see? Check (✓) all the correct answers. Then discuss your answers with a partner. Point to sentences in the text that helped you find your answer.

In the conclusion, the writer _____.

_____ returns to the main idea(s)

_____ gives an opinion

_____ comments on the future

↳ Go to **MyEnglishLab** for more skill practice.

CONNECT THE READINGS

ORGANIZE

Work with a partner. Fill in the information from each reading in the chart.

> **USE YOUR NOTES**
>
> Use your notes from Reading One and the information from Reading Two to complete the chart.

	Ronnie Elkhouly	Evan Taschen
1. What is he learning before he joins the professional world?	how to live in the spotlight	
2. Where or how is he learning these lessons?		
3. What are some difficulties that young pro players might have?		

SYNTHESIZE

Work with a partner. Complete the sentences with information from the chart.

For a young player who goes pro, there are some difficulties. First, _____
_____ . Also, _____
_____ .

Players need to learn more than a sport to go pro. They need to learn _____
_____ . They also need to
_____ .

Where can they learn these things? They need to go _____
_____ . Another idea is _____
_____ .

Go to **MyEnglishLab** to check what you learned.

178   UNIT 8

3 FOCUS ON WRITING

VOCABULARY

REVIEW

Cross out one word, phrase, or sentence in each item that does not make sense.

1. Joe was a really good (cooking / running / basketball) **coach**.
2. I think that Kelly **earns** (a good job / good grades in school / a lot of money).
3. The girl who takes care of our children is only 15, but she is **mature**. (She knows what to do in an emergency. / She stays calm if the kids are angry. / She talks to her boyfriend on the phone while she babysits.)
4. I want to have a big party after I **graduate** from (the supermarket / college / high school).
5. Jennifer is a very **responsible** worker. When you ask her to do something, she (forgets / does it well / makes sure the job is finished).
6. Aisha has great **talent** for (singing / walking / tennis).
7. After I graduated from high school, my family **recommended** that I (go to college / get a job / do my homework).
8. Maresa has **experience** as a pro golfer. (She can give advice to young golfers. / She doesn't like playing professional golf. / She knows how to live in the spotlight.)
9. Scott had some **difficulties** after he became a pro basketball player. (He didn't know how to deal with the media. / He hurt his arm and couldn't play any more. / He became more mature.)
10. Scott also didn't know how to **deal with** the media. (He got angry with their questions. / He played basketball every day. / He got upset about their comments about him.)
11. Lydia was upset about the media's (untrue / expensive / negative) **comments**.

EXPAND

1 Study the sports idioms. There is one example from sports and another from everyday school life for each one.

hog the (ball): keep the (ball) to yourself, control use of something, not share (something) with your group or teammates

Mary doesn't hog the ball. She passes the ball to her teammates when necessary.

Mary doesn't hog the paint in art class. She shares with other students.

call the shots: make all the decisions for a group

Listen to the coach. He calls all the shots.

Bill is our class president. He calls all the shots on the student council.

get the ball rolling: start something, like a conversation between people

Let's get the ball rolling, team. Go out on the field and win this game!

Let's get the ball rolling, class. First, let's talk about last night's homework.

be / get on the ball: be / become intelligent, focused, ready to act

On the tennis court, Vincent is always on the ball. He thinks only about the match.

Vincent! Wake up. Get on the ball! Pay attention! We are on page 204.

be a team player: work well with other people on a team or group members; cooperate with other people

If you want to play on this team, you have to be a team player. Don't hog the ball and don't try to be a star.

If you want an "A" on your group project in this class, you have to be a team player.

2 Match the situations with the correct responses.

Situations

1. Bryan always listens carefully and thinks about his group's opinions. You can say: _____

2. You are working with a group of classmates. Your assignment is to discuss why Ronnie Elkhouly should or should not turn pro. You are the group leader. To begin, you say: _____

3. You want to try to score a goal, but your teammate does not pass the ball to you or anyone. You say to your teammate: _____

4. You forgot your mother's birthday, but your secretary remembered. She sent your mother some flowers. You say: _____

5. You are the captain of the soccer team, and one of your teammates isn't listening to your instruction. You tell him: _____

Responses

a. "Hey, Jimmy. Don't hog the ball!"

b. "He's a real team player."

c. "Thanks for doing that for me, Dana. You are always on the ball."

d. "OK, who wants to get the ball rolling? Debbie, how about you?"

e. "I call all the shots during the game."

CREATE

3 **APPLY** Study the pictures. What are the people saying? Write their words on the line. Use the vocabulary from Expand.

Teacher: _____

Student (We have to work together.): _____

Student (Bob, you write the report. Karen, you give the oral presentation.): _____

Compare your answers with a partner's. Explain your choices.

Go to the **Pearson Practice English App** or **MyEnglishLab** for more vocabulary practice.

GRAMMAR FOR WRITING

1 Read each statement. Then choose the sentence that represents the meaning of the statement.

1. Some people think Elkhouly is **very mature** for his age.
   a. Elkhouly is less mature than other kids his age.
   b. Elkhouly is more mature than other kids his age.

2. Elkhouly is **too young** to play pro baseball in Japan.
   a. At his age, Elkhouly can't play pro baseball in Japan.
   b. At his age, Elkhouly can play pro baseball in Japan.

3. Kwasi Rodland is **too old** to play with the NBA.
   a. Rodland can't play with the NBA.
   b. Rodland can play with the NBA.

4. Kwasi Rodland is not **too old** to teach younger players.
   a. Rodland can't teach younger players.
   b. Rodland can teach younger players.

5. The teachers think Elkhouly is **mature enough** to play professional baseball.
   a. They think it's not OK for him to play professional baseball.
   b. They think it's OK for him to play professional baseball.

6. Evan Taschen is **old enough** to join the NBA.
   a. At his age, Taschen can't play in the NBA.
   b. At his age, Taschen can play in the NBA.

7. Many people think that Elkhouly is not **mature enough** to turn pro.
   a. They think it's not OK for Elkhouly to turn pro at his age.
   b. They think it's OK for Elkhouly to turn pro at his age.

Very, Too, and Enough

Use **very** before an adjective to make the adjective stronger. *Very* makes a positive adjective more positive. It makes a negative adjective more negative.

[adjective]
That car is **very beautiful.** I love it!

[adjective]
That car is **very expensive.** I'm not sure if I should spend so much.

Use **too** before an adjective to show a problem.

[adjective]
That car is **too expensive** for me to buy. I'll buy a less expensive one.

Use **enough** after an adjective or before a noun.

[adjective]
The yellow car isn't **fast enough** for me to buy. I think I'll buy the red one.

Use **enough** to say something about "amount."

[noun]
I have **enough money** to buy the red car,

[noun]
but I don't have **enough money** to buy the yellow one. I'll buy the red one.

These sentences have the same meaning: The yellow car is **too expensive** for me to buy. I don't have **enough money** to buy the yellow car.

These sentences also have the same meaning: The red car isn't **too expensive.** I have **enough money** to buy the red one.

2 Put the words in order to make sentences.

1. Kwasi Rodland / basketball / too / is / play / to / old / pro

   Kwasi Roland is too old to play pro basketball.

2. a / is / Joe / musician / talented / very

   _____

3. basketball / tall / to / is / play / enough / Kevin

   _____

4. enough / drive / not / is / Jamie / old / to

   _____

(continued on next page)

5. pick up / Sally / not / is / strong / enough / to / the box

   _____

6. Martina / win / at / Wimbledon / enough / was / to / good

   _____

3 Study the picture. Finish the sentences with the words provided. For the last two, write your own sentence about Ayala. Use *too* or *enough*.

1. Jeff / short <u>Jeff is too short to ride The Sled.</u>
2. Jeff / young _____
3. Jeff / heavy _____
4. Charlie / tall _____
5. Charlie / heavy _____
6. Charlie / old _____
7. Ayala _____
8. Ayala _____

4 **APPLY** Answer the questions with *too* or *enough*.

1. What are some things that you are too old to do now?

   _____

   _____

2. What are some things that you are not old enough to do yet?

   _____

   _____

Go to the **Pearson Practice English App** or **MyEnglishLab** for more grammar practice. Check what you learned in **MyEnglishLab**.

FINAL WRITING TASK: Opinion Paragraph APPLY

In this unit, you read about two young athletes. Now read the short newspaper article about another young player, Diana Verdejo.

San Rafael Observer, June 19, 2019

12-Year-Old Will Play Pro

Diana Verdejo loves golf, and she has a lot of talent. Diana is just 12 years old, but coaches call her every year because they want her to be on their teams. Now, professional coaches are calling because they want her to get ready for their professional teams. Diana knows that some young athletes turn pro at 14. Diana's parents say that they do not feel worried that she is too young to think about becoming a professional. They want her to do what she loves.

You are going to *write a paragraph expressing your opinion* about this young athlete and her plan to turn pro at age 12. Use the vocabulary and grammar from the unit.

For an alternative writing topic, see page 189.

PREPARE TO WRITE: Brainstorm

To help you plan your paragraph, you are going to brainstorm as a prewriting activity.

Work with a partner. Make a list of the pros and cons of becoming a pro athlete at a young age. Think about Ronnie Elkhouly and Evan Taschen. Add your own ideas. Write the benefits in the (+) column on the left and the drawbacks in the (−) column on the right.

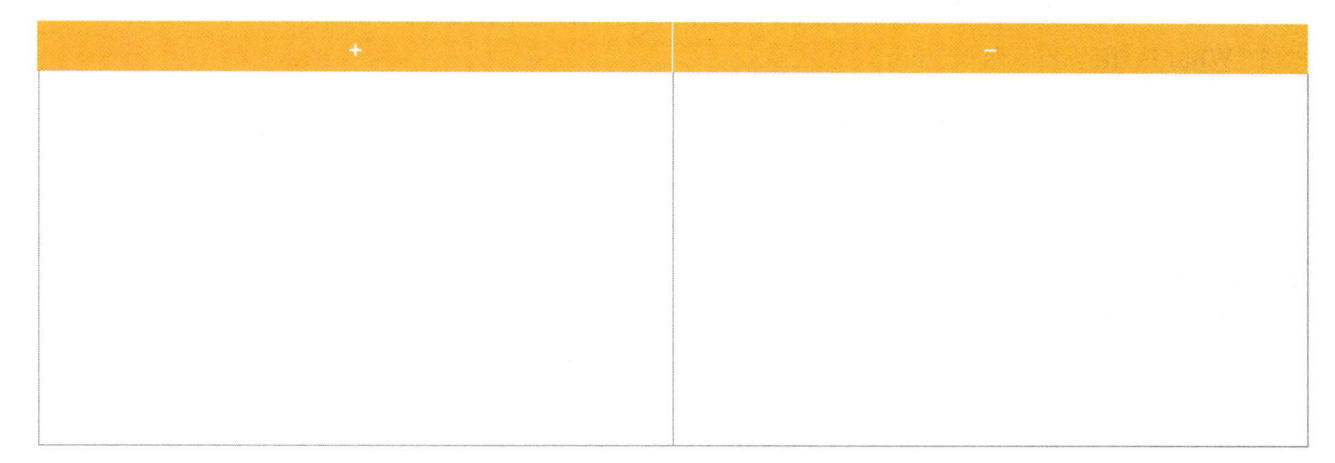

+	−

Look at the two columns. What's your opinion about Diana Verdejo?

WRITE: An Opinion Paragraph

In an opinion paragraph, you express your personal ideas about a topic. Like other paragraphs, an opinion paragraph begins with a topic sentence. The topic sentence gives your opinion. The other sentences give reasons for your opinion, or they explain or support your opinion.

To give an opinion, use the expressions in the chart.

In my opinion, + subject + verb + (the rest of the sentence)	**In my opinion,** Ronnie Elkhouly is old enough to be a professional athlete.
I think (that) + subject + *should* + main verb + (the rest of the sentence)	**I think that** Ronnie Elkhouly should become a professional athlete.
I (strongly) believe (that) + subject + verb + (the rest of the sentence) **Note:** Some people leave out **that**, especially when speaking.	**I (strongly) believe** Ronnie Elkhouly is old enough to be a professional athlete.

1 Read the paragraph. Then answer the questions.

> In my opinion, Ronnie Elkhouly is old enough to be a pro athlete. He is just 16 years old, but I think he is ready. One reason I think Ronnie is old enough is that he has support. He is not alone. Ronnie's teachers and coaches help him. They give him advice, and Ronnie listens. They gave him a job so he can learn to be responsible. Another reason is that playing pro is a good opportunity. Ronnie will earn a lot of money. In the future, he can spend his money on college. He can go to school any time, but he can play baseball only when he is young. For all these reasons, I think that Ronnie is ready.

1. What is the writer's opinion? _____

2. What reasons does the writer give for his or her opinion? _____

2 Write the first draft of your opinion paragraph about Diana Verdejo. Give reasons for your opinion. Use the chart on page 185 to help you write your paragraph.

REVISE

Write a Concluding Sentence

A concluding sentence is usually the last sentence of a paragraph. Often, the concluding sentence repeats or supports the main idea in the topic sentence. Sometimes the concluding sentence connects the main idea to the future.

Read the paragraph. Then read the four concluding sentences. Which answers fit?

   I think that young people should play sports. One reason is that sports are good exercise. Many kids prefer watching TV and using the Internet. They don't exercise, so they become unhealthy. If kids play sports, they will exercise and feel better. Another reason is that kids become mature when they play sports. Kids learn to work hard. They learn that they cannot be late.

Concluding Sentences:

a. For these reasons, sports are fun.
b. For these reasons, I think kids are good athletes.
c. For these reasons, I hope kids will play more sports.
d. For these reasons, sports are important for young people.

Sentence *a* does not fit because this idea is not in the paragraph.

Sentence *b* does not fit because it does not repeat or support the topic sentence (*"I think that young people should play sports."*).

Sentence *c* fits because it connects the main idea in the topic sentence to the future.

Sentence *d* fits because it supports the main idea in the topic sentence. This sentence says the main idea again in different words.

1 Write the letter of the concluding sentence next to the topic sentence. Then write what type of concluding sentence it is. Write Repetition or Future in the third column.

Topic Sentences	Concluding Sentences	Type of Concluding Sentences
____ 1. Evan is a talented athlete.	a. He wants to be more than just an athlete with expensive cars.	_____
____ 2. Evan got good advice from older players.	b. I believe that he will become a great pro player.	_____
____ 3. Evan cares about the important things in life.	c. He has learned important lessons.	_____

2 Read the paragraphs and write concluding sentences. Share your sentences with a partner.

1.
> In my opinion, running is the best sport. I think running is the best because I can run in all types of weather. When the weather is nice, I can run in a park and see interesting things. When the weather is bad, I can run in a gym.[1] Another reason is that running is relaxing. I can run alone and listen to music. I don't feel worried about anything.
>
> ---
> [1] **gym:** a large room where you do exercises or training

_____

_____

2.
> It is important for every athlete to have a good coach. Athletes need advice about playing. A good coach can teach the athlete how to play well. Another reason is that a good coach supports the athlete. The coach can say things like, "Keep working hard!" or "You can do it!" When athletes feel tired, a good coach helps them continue.

_____

_____

3 Now look at the first draft of your paragraph. Be sure you have a concluding sentence.

Go to **MyEnglishLab** for more skill practice.

EDIT: Writing the Final Draft

APPLY Write the final draft of your paragraph. Check your grammar, spelling, capitalization, and punctuation. Be sure to use some of the grammar and vocabulary from the unit. Use the checklist to help you write your final draft.

FINAL DRAFT CHECKLIST

- ☐ Did you express an opinion?
- ☐ Did you begin with a good topic sentence?
- ☐ Did you support your opinion with reasons?
- ☐ Did you use a concluding sentence? Does it support the topic sentence?
- ☐ Did you use *very, too,* and *enough*?
- ☐ Did you use vocabulary from the unit?

ALTERNATIVE WRITING TOPIC

APPLY Write a paragraph about a person who did something important at a young age. How did this person's life change as a result? Use vocabulary and grammar from the unit.

CHECK WHAT YOU'VE LEARNED

Check (✔) the outcomes you've met and vocabulary you've learned. Put an X next to the skills and vocabulary you still need to practice.

Learning Outcomes
- ☐ Infer priorities
- ☐ Take notes with an outline
- ☐ Identify the conclusion
- ☐ Use *very, too,* and *enough*
- ☐ Write a concluding sentence
- ☐ Write an opinion paragraph

Vocabulary
- ☐ coach
- ☐ comments AWL
- ☐ difficulties
- ☐ earned
- ☐ experience
- ☐ graduated
- ☐ mature AWL
- ☐ recommended
- ☐ responsible
- ☐ talent

Multi-word Units
- ☐ be a team player
- ☐ be / get on the ball
- ☐ call the shots
- ☐ deal with
- ☐ get the ball rolling
- ☐ hog the (ball)

Go to **MyEnglishLab** to watch a video about sports for non-jocks, access the Unit Project, and take the Unit 8 Achievement Test.

EXPAND VOCABULARY

UNIT 1
Vocabulary
be (am, is, are)
friend
garden (*n.*)
garden (*v.*)
live
love
walk (*n.*)
walk (*v.*)

UNIT 2
Vocabulary
dancer
dancing
dance (*v.*)
draw
energize
freedom
free (*adj.*)
free (*v.*)
paint (*n.*)
painter
paint (*v.*)
politician
post (*n.*)
posted
post (*v.*)
the public
publicize
sculptor
sculpting
sculpt
symbol AWL
symbolize AWL

UNIT 3
Vocabulary
collect
collector
collectible
condition
possession
excite
excited
exciting
sentimental
similar AWL
similarity AWL
sports
value
valuable

UNIT 4
Vocabulary
none

UNIT 5
Vocabulary
afraid of
embarrassed about
happy about
interested in
nervous about
relaxed about
scared of

UNIT 6
Vocabulary
none

UNIT 7
Vocabulary
grow up
sibling rivalry
take after

Multi-word Units
the black sheep
raise a family / children
it runs in the family

UNIT 8
Vocabulary
none

Multi-word Units
be a team player
be on the ball / get on the ball
call the shots
get the ball rolling
hog the ball

ACADEMIC WORD LIST VOCABULARY AWL

Words with an * are target vocabulary in the unit. The remainder of the words appear in context in the reading texts.

adult*	individual	role
benefit (*n.*)	institute	similar*
challenge (*n.*)	issue (*n.*)	similarity
comment* (*n.*)	item*	stressful*
community	job	symbol
computer	mature* (*adj.*)	symbolize
construct* (*v.*)	media	team
debate (*n.*)	normal*	topic
energetic*	physically	unique*
energy*	professional	volunteer (*v.*)
expert* (*n.*)	project (*n.*)	
final	relax*	
finally	relaxed*	
image	research (*n.*)	

GRAMMAR BOOK REFERENCES

NorthStar: Reading and Writing Level 1, Fourth Edition	Focus on Grammar, Level 1, Fifth Edition	Azar's Basic English Grammar, Fourth Edition
Unit 1 Present tense of *Be* and *Have*	Unit 3 Present of *Be*: Statements Unit 5 Present of *Be*: Yes/No Questions, Questions with Who and What	Chapter 1 Using *Be* Chapter 2 Using *Have* Chapter 3 Using the Simple Present: 3-1, 3-8, 3-9, 3-10, 3-11
Unit 2 Simple past of *Be* and *Have*	Part 3 *Be*: Past	Chapter 1 Using *Be* Chapter 2 Using *Have* Chapter 8 Expressing Past Time: 8-1, 8-2, 8-3
Unit 3 Simple Present	Unit 3 Present of *Be*: Statements Unit 10 Simple Present: Statements Unit 11 Simple Present: Yes/No Questions Unit 12 Simple Present: *Wh-* Questions	Chapter 15 Making Comparisons: 15-1
Unit 4 *There is / There are*	Unit 1 *There is / There are*	Chapter 5 Talking About the Present: 5–4, 5–5
Unit 5 *Can / May / Might / Will*	Unit 19 *Can* and *Can't*	Chapter 11 Expressing Future Time: 11-1, 11-2 Chapter 12 Modals, Part 1: 12-1, 12-2, 12-3
Unit 6 Simple Past	Part 8 Simple Past	Chapter 8 Expressing Past Time, Part 1
Unit 7 Comparative Adjectives	Unit 15 Comparative Adjectives	Chapter 15 Making Comparisons: 15-1
Unit 8 *Very / Too / Enough*	Unit 14 Adjectives	Chapter 12 Using *Very* and *Too* + Adjective: 12-7

CREDITS

VIDEO CREDITS

Unit 1: AP/BO Clips
Unit 2: ABC News Internet Ventures
Unit 3: ABC News Internet Ventures
Unit 4: ABC News Internet Ventures
Unit 5: Neuro Transmissions/BO Clips
Unit 6: ABC News Internet Ventures
Unit 7: ABC News Internet Ventures
Unit 8: ABC News Internet Ventures

PHOTO CREDITS

Cover
Jag_cz/Shutterstock (main); Hallojulie/Shutterstock (top).

Frontmatter
Page vi: Oneinchpunch/Shutterstock; vii (p. 4): Kummeleon/123RF; vii (p. 5): Pidjoe/iStock Unreleased/Getty Images; vii (p. 6): Francois Roux/Shutterstock; vii (p. 10): Mairo Cinquetti/NurPhoto/Getty Images; viii (p. 8): MikeDotta/Shutterstock; ix (p. 14): iMoved Studio/Shutterstock; ix (photo on cell phone): Oneinchpunch/Shutterstock; x: Engin Korkmaz/123RF; xiv (Unit 1 opener): Oneinchpunch/Shutterstock; xiv (Unit 2 opener): DisobeyArt/Shutterstock; xv (Unit 3 opener): Arcansel/Shutterstock; xv (Unit 4 opener): Rawpixel.com/Shutterstock; xvi (Unit 5 opener): Voit Svitlana/Shutterstock; xvi (Unit 6 opener): Bettmann/Getty Images; xvii (Unit 7 opener): Shutterstock; xvii (Unit 8 opener): Sergey Nivens/Shutterstock.

Unit 1
Page 2–3: Oneinchpunch/Shutterstock; 4: Kummeleon/123RF; 5: Pidjoe/iStock Unreleased/Getty Images; 6–7: Francois Roux/Shutterstock; 8–9: MikeDotta/Shutterstock; 10: Mairo Cinquetti/NurPhoto/Getty Images; 14–15: IMoved Studio/Shutterstock; 18: Julief514/123RF; 19: Moomusician/Shutterstock; 20: Engin Korkmaz/123RF.

Unit 2
Page 26–27: DisobeyArt/Shutterstock; 28 (center): Vasiliy Koval/Shutterstock; 28 (right): 3LH/SuperStock; 29 (left): Arte & Immagini srl/Vincenzo Fontana/Corbis Historical/Getty Images; 29 (right): Tala-Natali/Shutterstock; 30: Allan Tannenbaum/Polaris/Newscom; 31 (left): Untitled, 1984 © Keith Haring Foundation. Used by permission; 31 (right): Untitled (from the Icons series), 1990 (Radiant Baby) © Keith Haring Foundation. Used by permission; 34 (left): Free South Africa, 1985 © Keith Haring Foundation. Used by permission; 34 (right): Stop Aids, 1989 © Keith Haring Foundation. Used by permission; 38 (left): Untitled (from the Icons series), 1990 (Radiant Baby) © Keith Haring Foundation. Used by permission; 38 (center, left): Untitled, 1984 © Keith Haring Foundation. Used by permission; 38 (center, right): Stop Aids, 1989 © Keith Haring Foundation. Used by permission; 38 (right): Free South Africa, 1985 © Keith Haring Foundation. Used by permission; 46–47: Chamille White/Shutterstock.

Unit 3
Page 50–51: Arcansel/Shutterstock; 52: NaughtyNut/Shutterstock; 53 (top): Jackhollingsworth.com/Shutterstock; 53 (bottom): Everett Collection/Shutterstock; 54 (top, left): Jackhollingsworth.com/Shutterstock; 54 (top, right): 9246263575/Shuttersock; 54 (bottom): MimosaPhotography/Alamy Stock Photo; 57: Nampix/Shutterstock; 58: Peter Beck/Corbis/Getty Images; 61: Suzanne Tucker/Shutterstock; 62: Wk1003mike/Shutterstock.

Unit 4
Page 70–71: Rawpixel.com/Shutterstock; 72–73: Artem Podporin/Shutterstock; 74 (top): Rudmer Zwerver/Shutterstock; 74 (bottom): Riekephotos/Shutterstock; 79 (furniture): George Dolgikh/Shutterstock; 79 (clothing): Amy Rene/Shutterstock; 79 (jewelry): AleksandrN/Shutterstock; 79 (gift wrap): Irina Bort/Shutterstock; 83: Beeboys/Shutterstock; 84: AnjelikaGr/Shutterstock.

Unit 5
Page 94–95: Voit Svitlana/Shutterstock; 98 (top): XONIX/Shutterstock; 98 (bottom): Alexsander Isachenko/Shutterstock; 101: Twin Design/Shutterstock; 107: Andrea Raffin/Shutterstock; 116: Dan Ross/Shutterstock.

Unit 6
Page 118–119: Bettmann/Getty Images; 126 (left): Steven Day/AP images; 126 (right): Lisa O'Connor/ZUMA Press, Inc./Alamy Stock Photo; 127: Anton Podoshvin/123RF; 131: Everett Historical/Shutterstock; 135: Jordan Siemens/Photodisc/Getty Images; 139: Alexander Gordeyev/Shutterstock; 140: Rad K/Shutterstock.

Unit 7
Page 142–143: Shutterstock; 145: Shutterstock; 146: Chronicler/Shutterstock; 149: Lucidio Studio, Inc./Moment/Getty Images; 154: Twinsterphoto/Shutterstock; 159: Wakeham/Splash News/Newscom.

Unit 8
Page 166–167: Sergey Nivens/Shutterstock; 168 (Pele): George Tiedemann/Sports Illustrated/Getty Images; 168 (Martina Hingis): Peter Parks/AFP/Getty Images; 168 (Chloe Kim): Nippon News/Hiroyuki Sato/AFLO/Alamy Stock Photo; 170 (baseball player): JLBarranco/E+/Getty Images; 170 (stadium background): Margie Hurwich/Shutterstock; 173: Michael Dwyer/Alamy Stock Photo; 174: Larry Williams/Corbis/Getty Images; 176: DarioZg/Shutterstock; 179: Taka1022/Shutterstock; 182–183: Aaron Amat/Shutterstock; 183 (left): Gustavo Fadel/Shutterstock; 183 (right): Dinodia Photos/Alamy Stock Photo.

ILLUSTRATION CREDITS

Aphik Diseño, ElectraGraphics, Paul Hampson, Dusan Petriçic, Gary Torrisi, Deborah White

NOTES

NOTES

NOTES

NOTES

NOTES

NOTES

NOTES

NOTES

NOTES

NOTES

NOTES

NOTES

NOTES